☀ The Mystery and Magic Series ☀

Heroes
and
Heroines

Robert Ingpen & Molly Perham

DRAGON'S WORLD

CHILDREN'S BOOKS

Dragon's World Ltd
Limpsfield
Surrey RH8 0DY
Great Britain

First published by Dragon's World Ltd, 1995

Editor: Diana Briscoe
Designer: Megra Mitchell
Design Assistants:
Karen Ferguson
Victoria Furbisher
Art Director: John Strange
Editorial Director: Pippa Rubinstein

British Library Cataloguing in Publication Data
The catalogue record for this book is available from the British Library.

ISBN 1 85028 300 1

Typeset by Dragon's World Ltd in Caslon, Century Old Style and Helvetica.
Printed in Italy

✳ Contents ✳

✳ Contents ✳

All around the world, famous heroes and heroines stride through the pages of legend. No one knows whether they are purely legendary figures, or whether they are based on people who actually lived. Over the centuries myths and real events have merged into heroic sagas of dangerous adventures, of battles with monsters and giants, and of rescuing victims in distress.

Some heroes like Rama and Charlemagne were revered as ideal rulers – strong, just, benevolent and wise – and represent the ideals of bravery and chivalry. Valiant warriors, such as Lady Bradamante of France or Rustam of Persia fought for their countries against foreign tyranny and invasion.

The Greek heroes Odysseus and Jason undertook long journeys during which they encountered all kinds of fearsome dangers. Others, like Brynhild, faced impossible problems of honour. In India, many heroes are considered to be gods who have been reborn on earth.

Heroes and heroines are marked out for greatness from the day they are born. They may possess superhuman strength, or magical powers. Sometimes their birth is preceded by strange events, or dangers and trials beset them as a child. But one thing is sure: good always triumphs over evil.

Molly Perham

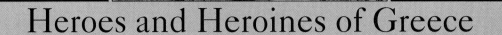

Heroes and Heroines of Greece

The ancient Greeks told many stories of heroic men and women who, although they were not actual gods, had superhuman powers. Some of these may originally have been based on real people whose deeds gradually became much exaggerated. The Greeks believed that they were taken after death to a beautiful land called Elysium. This was not actually in heaven, but far away to the west, at the world's end. In Elysium, the weather was always perfect and the Greeks spent their time enjoying open-air sports, feasts and festivals.

The Twelve Labours of Heracles

The myths told by the ancient Greeks are well known in the Western world. Our knowledge of them has been helped by the many inscriptions and documents that have been found all over the ancient Greek world.

Heracles was the son of Zeus and a mortal princess called Alcmene. When Zeus's wife Hera heard about Heracles' birth she was extremely jealous and sent two snakes to kill the child in his cradle. But the baby Heracles was already so strong that he strangled the snakes with his own hands.

Heracles grew up to be a mighty warrior and hunter, but Hera still hated him. She caused Heracles to be seized with a madness, during which he killed his wife Megara and their children. To make amends, the oracle at Delphi told Heracles to complete twelve tasks for King Eurystheus of Tiryns.

At this time, the valley of Nemea was inhabited by a fierce lion that had eaten all the hunters who had been sent to capture it. King Eurystheus ordered Heracles to bring him the skin of the lion. Heracles went to the lion's den, seized the animal and strangled it, just as he had strangled the serpents when he was a baby.

Heracles' next labour was to kill the Hydra, a monster that ravaged the country of Argos. Accompanied by his faithful servant Iolaus, Heracles set off to find the monster in the swamp where it lived. The Hydra had nine heads, and its middle head was immortal.

Heracles attacked the monster savagely, but each time he struck off one head, two more heads grew in its place. Eventually, to stop new heads growing, Iolaus held a burning torch to each of the nine necks as its head fell. In this way, they were able to overcome the Hydra,

and finally bury the monster's ninth immortal head under a huge rock.

For his third task, Heracles was sent to capture one of the five golden-horned stags that were sacred to Artemis the huntress. Artemis had harnessed four of the stags to her chariot, while a fifth wandered free in the hills of Arcadia, and no one dared touch it. Heracles pursued the stag for a whole year until eventually he caught it.

As he was bringing the animal to Eurystheus at Tiryns, Artemis greeted him angrily. 'How dare you carry off my hind!' she cried.

When Heracles explained that he had only captured the stag at Eurystheus' command, Artemis forgave him and said, 'Go and show the hind to Eurystheus and then return it to Arcadia. Otherwise Eurystheus will feel my anger!'

Heracles delivered her message, and Eurystheus sighed with relief when the golden-horned stag had been returned to its immortal owner. 'Now bring me the wild boar of Erymanthus,' he commanded Heracles. 'And make sure you bring it alive, as it belongs to Apollo, the twin brother of Artemis.' The boar lived on a snow-covered mountainside, so Heracles was able to follow its tracks and chase the animal into a deep snowdrift. Quickly tying its legs with a rope, Heracles slung the boar over his shoulder and took it to Eurystheus. The King was so terrified at the sight of the fierce beast that he jumped into a large brass pot and hid until Heracles had taken it away again.

Heracles' fifth labour was to clean out the stables belonging to King Augeas, in which three thousand oxen lived. The stables had not been cleaned for thirty years, and Heracles was ordered to perform the task in just one day. He managed to do it by building a dam across a nearby river and diverting the water so that it flowed through the stables.

For his sixth labour, Heracles was told to go and chase off the Stymphalian birds. These belonged to the war god, Ares, and they lived in the thick forest around Lake Stymphalus. The birds had brass claws with which they stripped all the trees of fruit, and beaks so sharp that they could pierce a man's armour.

On his way through the forest, Heracles met Athene, who gave him a pair of castanets made of bronze. With these, Heracles made such a fearsome noise that the birds flew off shrieking. He shot some of them down with poisoned arrows, and carried them back to show Eurystheus.

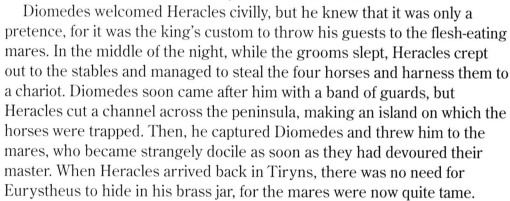

Heracles' seventh task was to capture the Cretan bull, father of the terrible Minotaur. Heracles sailed to the island of Crete, where he was warmly welcomed by King Minos at the palace of Knossos. After all his other exploits, Heracles had no trouble catching the bull. He took the creature back to Greece and let it loose in Tiryns. As soon as Eurystheus saw the bull he jumped into the brass pot again and stayed there for several days.

When the King had recovered from his fright, he set Heracles his eighth labour. 'Go north into Thrace and bring back the four mares of King Diomedes,' he ordered. 'But be sure you tame them before you bring them back to Tiryns, because they feed on human flesh.'

Diomedes welcomed Heracles civilly, but he knew that it was only a pretence, for it was the king's custom to throw his guests to the flesh-eating mares. In the middle of the night, while the grooms slept, Heracles crept out to the stables and managed to steal the four horses and harness them to a chariot. Diomedes soon came after him with a band of guards, but Heracles cut a channel across the peninsula, making an island on which the horses were trapped. Then, he captured Diomedes and threw him to the mares, who became strangely docile as soon as they had devoured their master. When Heracles arrived back in Tiryns, there was no need for Eurystheus to hide in his brass jar, for the mares were now quite tame.

Heracles was now given his ninth task. Admete, the daughter of Eurystheus, longed to own the golden girdle that belonged to Hippolyta, Queen of the Amazons. The girdle had been given to Hippolyta by Ares, and gave its wearer strength in battle. Eurystheus ordered Heracles to get the girdle for Admete.

The Amazons were a warlike race of women who brought up only female children. Boy children were either sent away or put to death. On this adventure, Heracles was accompanied by nine companions. When they reached the land of the Amazons, Hippolyta received them kindly and agreed to give Heracles the girdle. But Hera, furious that he was accomplishing this task so easily, disguised herself as an Amazon and persuaded the other women that Heracles was planning to carry off the Queen. They armed themselves and came after him. Heracles was more than able to defend himself, and Hippolyta was killed in the skirmish.

Heracles was then told to fetch the oxen of Geryon, a monster with three bodies, from the island of Erytheia. To get there, he broke a mountain in two, forming the Straits of Gibraltar, which in ancient times were known as the Pillars of Heracles.

Geryon was guarded by the giant Eurytion and his two-headed dog, but Heracles killed them both and brought the oxen safely to Tiryns.

Heracles' eleventh labour was to get the three Golden Apples of the Hesperides, which Hera had received as a wedding gift. This was a particularly difficult task, because no one knew where to find the apples. After searching throughout the world, Heracles finally arrived at Mount Atlas in Africa. Atlas, who bore the weight of the heavens on his shoulders, was the father of the three Hesperides nymphs. Heracles took the heavens on to his own shoulders while Atlas went off to get the apples from his daughters. Then, Atlas took the weight back once more, and Heracles returned to Tiryns with the apples.

The twelfth and last of Heracles' labours was to fetch the three-headed dog Cerberus who guarded the gates of hell. Pluto, the god of the underworld, gave Heracles his permission to carry the beast to the upper air, provided that he could do so without the use of weapons. With the messenger god Hermes as his guide, Heracles journeyed through the realms of darkness, seized the monster and took it to Eurystheus, who hid in the pot yet again.

So Heracles returned to Tiryns for the last time, for his labours were now over. On his way home, he stopped at the house of his friend Pittheus, and threw his lion-skin over a chair. Pittheus' seven year-old grandson, Theseus, took a sword and attacked it, thinking it was alive.

Heracles laughed encouragingly. 'You will be following in my footsteps before long,' he cried. And so it was to be for Theseus grew up to be one of the greatest heroes of ancient Greece.

Jason and the Golden Fleece

The King of Thessaly had two children called Phrixus and Helle. Their stepmother hated them and wanted them killed, but they were saved by a present that their real mother had given them, a wonderful ram with a golden fleece. The ram carried the children on its back across the straits that divide Europe and Asia.

Helle slipped from the ram's back and fell into the Black Sea, but Phrixus landed safely at Colchis on the eastern shore. To give thanks for his escape, Phrixus sacrificed the ram to Zeus and hung its golden fleece in a grove, where it was guarded by a fierce dragon that never slept.

When the King of Thessaly died, his nephew Aeson succeeded him, but was soon driven out by his stepbrother Pelias. Aeson had a son named Jason, whom he had sent away to be brought up by the centaur Chiron.

When Jason was grown up, he came to Pelias and demanded the return of his father's kingdom. Pelias promised that Jason could have the kingdom if he brought back the Golden Fleece from Colchis.

Jason agreed to go on this quest, and soon fifty heroes from all parts of Greece gathered to set sail with him in his ship, the *Argo*. After many adventures, the *Argo* with its crew, called the Argonauts, reached Colchis.

'I will give you the Golden Fleece if you can plough a field with my pair of fire-breathing bulls and sow it with dragons' teeth,' said Aeetes, the King of Colchis. Aeetes knew that a crop of armed warriors would spring up from the teeth and turn their swords against Jason.

While preparations were being made for the task, Jason met and fell in love with Medea, the King's daughter. Medea was a sorceress, and she gave Jason a charm that would protect him against the fire-breathing bulls and armed warriors.

At the appointed time, the people of Colchis assembled on a nearby hillside to watch the spectacle, while the King took his royal seat. The two bulls rushed on to the field, breathing fire from their nostrils, and burning up grass and bushes as they passed.

Everyone shrank back at their approach, but Jason walked boldly forward and patted the bulls' necks to soothe them. Then he slipped on the yoke and harnessed the bulls to the plough.

The Colchians watched with amazement as Jason guided the plough to make furrows and then sowed the dragons' teeth.

Within seconds, a crop of armed warriors sprang up and brandished their weapons at Jason. For a time, he kept them at bay with his sword and shield, but then he resorted to the trick that Medea had taught him.

Seizing a stone, he threw it into the middle of the group of warriors. They immediately turned against each other, and soon not one was left alive. The Argonauts cheered their hero, and Medea sat proud and happy at her father's side.

Jason, having won the right to the Golden Fleece, now had to pass by the dragon to get it. Once more, Medea came to his aid. She gave him a powerful oil which Jason sprinkled near the monster. At the smell, the dragon stood motionless for a moment, then shut the great eyes that had never before been known to close and fell fast asleep.

Jason seized the Golden Fleece, and the Greeks hastened back to the *Argo*, taking Medea with them. The triumphant Argonauts sailed back to Thessaly, where Jason delivered the fleece to Pelias and at last claimed his rightful throne.

Atalanta the Huntress

Every city of ancient Greece had its own myths, heroes and religious festivals, and from these developed a huge collection of stories in which the many different characters were interlinked. Atalanta came from Arcadia and was the heroine of several ancient Greek stories.

Atalanta was born a princess, but her father King Iasus was so disappointed that she was not a son that he left her out on a hillside to die. A bear brought the baby girl up with her own cubs, and the goddess Artemis taught Atalanta to be a huntress and allowed her to join the nymphs who were her followers.

Meleager was one of the young men who had sailed with Jason in the *Argo* in search of the Golden Fleece. During the voyage, he met and fell in love with Atalanta, but she refused his hand because she had sworn never to marry. When Meleager returned home to Calydon, he found that a savage boar was laying waste to all the land, destroying the crops and killing anyone who tried to capture it. It had been sent by the goddess Artemis, who had been offended because Meleager's father had failed to make a sacrifice to her. Meleager sent for some of his Argonaut friends to help him in the hunt, including Atalanta.

The huntress came willingly, but Meleager's uncles, Phexippus and Toxeus, protested when they saw her. 'Do you expect us to go hunting with a woman!' they cried. 'She should be sitting at her loom, not joining with men in the chase.'

However, while the men vigorously threw their spears and missed, Atalanta quietly drew her bow and sent an arrow straight into the boar's head. This partly subdued the great beast but did not kill it, and several more of the hunters lost their lives in trying to complete the task.

At last, Meleager managed to finish it off, and when he had skinned the boar he presented Atalanta with the animal's head and hide, saying 'Huntress, you were the first to wound the boar, so you deserve the glory more than I myself or any of the others.'

Phexippus and Toxeus were so furious at this that they grabbed the spoils from Atalanta and called her a shameless hussy. Then Meleager lost his temper and killed both his uncles on the spot.

The great boar hunt ended in sadness and tragedy, but King Iasus heard of Atalanta's part in the battle and claimed her as his daughter. He begged Atalanta to choose a husband so that they could rule after him and produce an heir.

Atalanta was worried by this request because the Oracle at Delphi had warned her against marriage. 'Father, I will consent on one condition. I will marry any man who can beat me in a race,' said Atalanta. 'But any man who tries and is beaten will pay with his life.'

Several young men challenged the Princess, but none could run faster than she could. As Atalanta overtook her suitors on the race-course, she speared them in the back.

One day, however, she was challenged by Hippomenes, who was a favourite of Aphrodite. The goddess of love was angry with Atalanta for refusing love, so she gave Hippomenes the three Golden Apples that Heracles had brought from the Garden of the Nymphs of the Hesperides.

During the race, Hippomenes threw them down one by one in front of Atalanta. These Golden Apples were so lovely that Atalanta could not resist stopping to pick them up. That was how Hippomenes arrived at the finishing post first and won Atalanta as his wife.

Theseus and the Minotaur

In Greek mythology Theseus is particularly honoured for bringing all the different towns and villages of Attica, the region around Athens, under a single ruler as a unified state. The tragic story of Phaedra of Crete, his second wife, is told in a play called *Hippolytus*, written by the Greek dramatist Euripides.

O ne of the greatest heroes of ancient Greece was Theseus, son of Aegeus, King of Athens. Theseus was born and brought up in his grandfather's palace at Troezene. Only when he reached manhood did he set out on the journey to his father's palace in Athens. On the way, Theseus proved his strength and valour by overcoming many dangers.

Having conquered all the perils of the journey, Theseus reached Athens at last. However, instead of rejoicing in their hero's triumph, the Athenians were in a state of great distress. Each year, Athens had to send a tribute of seven youths and seven maidens to Minos, King of Crete. There, the young people were devoured by the Minotaur, a monster with a bull's body and a human head. This fearsome beast was kept in a labyrinth full of winding passages and turnings. Once inside, it was impossible to find a way out.

When Theseus arrived in Athens, the time was approaching for the annual sacrifice. The youths and maidens were drawn by lot, but Theseus, in spite of his father's pleading, offered himself as one of the victims. He was determined to kill the Minotaur and save his countrymen from their terrible plight.

On the morning of their departure, Theseus joined the weeping group. They were all dressed in black, and the ship that took them had black sails. Theseus promised his father that if he were successful in killing the Minotaur, he would change the sails to white on his return journey.

In Crete, the youths and maidens were exhibited before King Minos in his palace at Knossos. The national sport of the Cretans, which also was part of their religion, was bull-leaping. This involved somersaulting and other athletic feats over the horns of one of the bulls that were sacred to the sea god, Poseidon. Theseus proved to be a champion at the art and performed feats seldom seen before in Crete.

Ariadne, the eldest daughter of the King, saw him performing and fell in love with Theseus. She gave him a spool of thread, and told him to tie one end of the thread to a stone as he entered the labyrinth and unwind it as he made his way through the maze. When he had found and killed the Minotaur, he could find his way back to the entrance by following the thread.

The Athenians clung together as they entered the dark, wet caves. Theseus unwound the thread as he had been instructed by Ariadne. Before long, they heard a tremendous bellowing and then the stamping of angry feet. Ordering his companions to hide behind some rocks, Theseus advanced alone to meet the Minotaur.

The monster caught sight of the

young man and charged forward to devour him. With one quick movement, Theseus stepped forward and plunged his sword deep into the Minotaur's chest. When they were sure it was dead, the others threw their arms joyfully around each other. Then, following the precious thread, they made their way out of the labyrinth.

The Athenians sailed for home, taking Ariadne with them. On the way, they stopped at the island of Naxos, where Theseus dreamed that Athene appeared to him and commanded him to abandon Ariadne. He woke his companions and sailed away, leaving Ariadne asleep on the island.

As the ship approached Athens, Theseus forgot to change the black sails for white ones. Aegeus, believing that his son was dead, threw himself into the sea and drowned. In this tragic way, Theseus became King of Athens.

The Trojan War

The blind Greek poet Homer wrote of the war between the Greeks and the Trojans in a long poem called the *Iliad*. This war actually took place four or five hundred years before Homer's time, in the 13th or 12th century BC. Many legends grew up about it later, so that no one now knows which things actually took place and which were made up by the storytellers.

Peleus, one of the men who had sailed with Jason on the *Argo*, married Thetis, the loveliest of the Nereides, or sea nymphs. All the gods and goddesses were invited to the wedding feast, with the exception of Eris, goddess of discord. Furious at this slight, she threw a golden apple among the guests. This apple bore the inscription 'For the fairest'.

Hera, Aphrodite and Athene each claimed the apple and were soon quarrelling bitterly. Zeus was not willing to decide such a difficult matter, so he sent the goddesses to Mount Ida, where Paris was tending his flocks. The goddesses gathered around the handsome shepherd, each offering to reward him if he gave her the prize. Hera promised Paris power and riches; Athene said she would bring him glory and fame; and Aphrodite vowed that he would have the most beautiful woman in the world as his wife. Paris chose Aphrodite and gave her the golden apple, thus making enemies of the other two goddesses.

◁ Aphrodite enlisted Ares, the god of war, on her side. Poseidon, god of the underworld, also favoured the Trojans. Apollo remained neutral, sometimes taking one side, sometimes the other. Zeus himself, though he loved the good King Priam, was also impartial.

Paris was the son of Priam, King of Troy, but he had been brought up in obscurity because an oracle had prophesied that he would one day bring ruin to the city. Under the protection of Aphrodite, Paris sailed for Sparta to claim his prize, the most beautiful woman in the world. This woman was Helen, the wife of Menelaus, King of Sparta.

Paris persuaded Helen to elope with him to Troy. Overcome by grief, Menelaus called upon all the chieftains of Greece to help him recover his wife. An army was quickly assembled, with Agamemnon, his brother, as commander-in-chief. Among the illustrious warriors were Ajax, Diomedes, Nestor, Odysseus and Achilles, the greatest of them all.

King Priam of Troy was old and weak, but his son Hector was a brave and noble young man. Hector had felt a presentiment of danger when his brother Paris brought Helen back to Troy. He knew that he must fight for his family, but grieved at the circumstances that had set hero against hero. The other principal warriors on the Trojan side were Aeneas, Deiphobus, Glaucus and Sarpedon.

After two years of preparation, the Greek fleet and army assembled and set out for Troy. For nine years, the two armies fought, neither side winning over the other. Achilles soon showed himself to be the bravest and most daring of the Greek warriors, but he quarrelled with Agamemnon and refused to go on fighting.

After this, the war went badly for the Greeks, and Patroclus, who was his best friend, persuaded Achilles to lend him his armour, hoping to deceive the Trojans into thinking that Achilles was once more fighting against them. Hector fought with Patroclus, thinking him to be Achilles, and killed him.

When Achilles learned of his friend's death he swore to avenge him. He rejoined the Greek army and fought so fiercely that the Trojans withdrew into the city, leaving Hector, who refused to retreat, alone on the battlefield. However, when Hector saw that he was facing the real Achilles, he was afraid and ran towards the city gates. Achilles ran faster and cut off his retreat. Three times they circled the walls, until Hector saw that escape was impossible and turned to fight. Achilles killed Hector with a thrust of his spear, and then in triumph dragged the body behind his chariot to the tomb of Patroclus.

With Hector's death, the Trojans suffered a serious defeat, but soon afterwards Paris shot a poisoned arrow at Achilles. Before Achilles was born, the Fates had told his mother that he would die young, so she had bathed him in the River Styx, whose magic waters were said to give protection from all wounds and diseases. But the waters did not touch the heel by which Achilles' mother had held him. The gods guided Paris's arrow to his heel, the one part of his body that was vulnerable. Achilles died from the wound.

The Greeks began to despair of ever conquering the city of Troy, and decided to resort to a trick. They pretended to be getting ready to abandon the siege, and most of the ships set sail with warriors on board. They did not head for home, however, but sailed to a nearby island where they hid in a harbour. The Greeks who were left behind built a huge wooden horse, which they filled with armed men and left in their camp. The remaining Greeks then sailed away.

When the Trojans saw that the Greek camp had disbanded and the fleet

had gone, they threw open the gates of the city and rushed out to look at the abandoned camp. They found the wooden horse and wondered what it could be. Some thought it should be carried back to the city and put on exhibition as a trophy of war, but others were afraid of it.

Lacoön, the priest of Poseidon, tried to warn the Trojans against it. 'Are you mad?' he exclaimed. 'Have you not seen enough of Greek trickery to be on your guard against it? I myself suspect the Greeks, even when they appear to be offering gifts.' As Lacoön was speaking, some Trojans appeared dragging a captive between them. They promised to spare his life if he answered their questions truthfully.

'My name is Sinon,' said the young Greek. 'My countrymen have abandoned me because I committed a trifling offence. The wooden horse is a peace offering to Athene. The gods told us that if you Trojans took possession of it, then we would lose the war. We have made the horse huge so that you cannot carry it into the city.'

On hearing this, the Trojans immediately began to drag the enormous horse into Troy. They placed it in the main square and spent the rest of the day celebrating and feasting. At last, exhausted from the festivities, they went to their homes and fell into their beds.

When the city was quiet, the armed men who were hidden in the body of the horse were let out by Sinon. They opened the gates of Troy and let in their companions, who had returned under cover of darkness. The Greeks set fire to the city, and the Trojans died in their beds. Troy had fallen. Menelaus hastened to the palace, found Helen and took her back to Sparta.

The story of the *Iliad* ends with the death of Hector, and it is from the *Odyssey* and later poems, such as the Roman poet Virgil's *Aeneid*, that we learn the fate of the other heroes.

How Aeneas escaped from Troy

The *Aeneid* is a long epic poem by the Roman poet Virgil, which was written about 20 BC, about one of the Trojan heroes called Aeneas. It tells how, after many adventures, Aeneas came to Italy and became the founder of the Roman people.

When the Greeks captured Troy and set it on fire, Aeneas, one of the Trojan warrior princes, fled from the leaping flames. His mother, Aphrodite the goddess of love, appeared to Aeneas and told him to leave the city at once and set out to look for a new home for the Trojan people.

Aeneas' wife had been killed during the siege, but the warrior managed to escape from the scene of destruction carrying his old father Anchises on his back and holding his young son by the hand.

Aeneas gathered together some companions and they set sail in twelve ships to look for a new land in which to settle. Their first landing was on the island of the Harpies, monsters who were half women and half birds.

The Trojans slew some of the cattle they found roaming over the plain, but no sooner had they started to eat than a flock of Harpies descended from the skies, seized the meat in their talons and flew away with it. Aeneas and his friends drew their swords to attack the Harpies, but their feathers were like armour and the warriors could not harm them.

The Trojans hurried to leave the island. They coasted along the shore of Sicily, past the country of the one-eyed Cyclops and between Scylla and Charybdis, the six-headed monster and the whirlpool which were so dangerous to sailors. On Sicily Aeneas' father died, and when the ships set sail again after the funeral, a great storm blew up, destroying most of the fleet. Aeneas' ship was driven on to the coast of Africa, near the city of Carthage.

Dido, the beautiful Queen of Carthage, fell in love with Aeneas and wanted him to share her kingdom. However Aeneas was determined to continue his search for a place to build a new city. He sailed away from her, and eventually reached Italy.

Here Aeneas met King Latinus, who promised the hand of his daughter Lavinia in marriage, although she was already engaged to Turnus, the prince of a tribe nearby. Turnus roused up all the nations of Italy to fight against Aeneas and the Trojans.

After several fierce battles Aeneas was victorious and killed Turnus in single combat. So he became the ruler of this new country – and from him and his followers, the Roman people were descended.

The Adventures of Odysseus

Homer's other great poem, the *Odyssey*, tells of the ten-year-long adventures of the Greek hero Odysseus (or Ulysses) on his way back to his home on the island of Ithaca after the fall of Troy.

W hen Troy had fallen, Odysseus and his men set sail for home. Before long the winds blew their ships off course, first to the land of the Lotus-eaters, then to the island of the cannibal Cyclops, called Polyphemus. After a narrow escape from Polyphemus' cave, the voyagers sailed on to visit Aeolus, the god of the winds, who gave Odysseus all the winds that might hinder him on his homeward course, tied up in a bag.

However his men, overcome with curiosity, opened the bag one night and let out the winds. A huge tempest destroyed all the ships except the one carrying Odysseus. That single ship, full of sorrowing and despairing men, next came to an island called Aeaea, ruled by the enchantress Circe. She could cast a spell that turned her victims into animals.

Odysseus ordered half his crew, under the leadership of Eurylochus, to go and ask for hospitality. As they approached the palace, the men heard soft music and a woman's voice singing. They eagerly followed Circe, all except Eurylochus, who suspected danger. He hid himself in a tall tree where he could look over the hedge and see what happened to his men.

Circe led the men to a banqueting table and served them wine until they were drunk, and food until they were stuffed like pigs. Before long, the seamen began to snort and snuffle like pigs, their noses turned into snouts and their ears grew large. Under Eurylochus' horrified gaze, the guzzling men were transformed into a herd of swine.

Eurylochus rushed back to tell Odysseus what had happened. As Odysseus was wondering how to rescue his men, Hermes, the messenger of the gods, appeared and gave him a sprig of the plant moly, which makes humans immune to enchantment. Thus protected, Odysseus was able to persuade Circe to free his men.

For seven years, the Greeks stayed on in Circe's palace, but then their desire to reach home became strong once more. Circe saw them sadly to their ship, and instructed them how to pass safely by the Sirens.

THE SIRENS

Ancient legends tell of the Sirens, sea nymphs who charmed sailors with their marvellous songs, until the men were irresistibly compelled to throw themselves into the sea.

Circe told Odysseus to fill the ears of his crew with wax so that they could not hear the Sirens' music, and to have himself bound to the mast with strong ropes. 'Warn your men,' she said, 'that no matter how much you beg to be released,

they must not untie you until the ship has passed the Sirens' island.'

It was just as well that Odysseus followed her advice, for when they reached the island, the music that came over the calm waters was so lovely that he struggled to get free.

The men, obedient to his orders, bound him still tighter until the music grew fainter and fainter, and faded into the distance.

SCYLLA AND CHARYBDIS

In a cave high up on a rocky cliff, near a narrow passage through which Odysseus' ship had to pass, lived the six-headed monster Scylla. She had once been a lovely water nymph, but when she spurned the love of Glaucus, a sea god, Circe had turned her into a monster. From each ship that passed, Scylla seized and ate six of the crew.

Near the cave where Scylla lived was a whirlpool called Charybdis. Three times a day, the water rushed into the whirlpool with such force that any ship coming near was sucked down into the depths.

Circe had warned Odysseus of these two dangers, but as he watched the dreadful whirlpool with anxious eyes, he was not on guard from Scylla's attack. Six snaky heads darted down, snatched six of his men from the deck of the ship, and bore them away to her den.

The Homecoming

The adventures that befell Odysseus on his way home from the siege of Troy delayed him for ten years. His home was on the island of Ithaca off the west coast of the Greek mainland, and it was here that his wife Penelope and son Telemachus were waiting for him.

Some neighbouring chieftains had taken over Odysseus' land on Ithaca, telling Penelope that her husband was dead and that she must choose a new husband from among them. Penelope put them off by insisting that she must finish weaving a shroud for Odysseus' old father before she decided who she would marry. She worked at the weaving every day, but every night she pulled her work to pieces so that it would never be finished.

It was a great relief to mother and son when the goddess Athene came, disguised as an old friend of Odysseus, and suggested that Telemachus should set out to seek news of his father. This postponed taking a decision still further, but Penelope's suitors were furious and they plotted to murder Telemachus when he returned.

After escaping from the perils of the Sirens and of Scylla and Charybdis, Odysseus and his ship had arrived at Thrinakia, the island of Hyperion, the god who drove the chariot of the Sun. His starving crew could not resist killing and roasting the cattle they found there. Hyperion, enraged, caused a shipwreck that destroyed many of the sailors and stranded Odysseus on the isle of Ogygia that belonged to the sea nymph Calypso.

Telemachus learned from Menelaus, King of Sparta, that Odysseus was detained on Ogygia by Calypso. The gods ordered Calypso to set him free, and once more Odysseus set sail, only to be wrecked again on the island of Scheria through the malice of Poseidon, who had favoured the Trojans.

Luckily for him, he was found and helped by Nausicaa, the King's daughter, who took him to her father's palace. There, to the King and his court, Odysseus told the story of all the adventures of his journey. King Alcinous was so moved by Odysseus' tale of disasters that he gave him a ship to enable him to return home, and sent his own men to sail it.

This time, Odysseus reached Ithaca safely, and the friendly sailors laid him gently on the sands, fast asleep. When he awoke, Athene warned Odysseus about Penelope's suitors and the plot to kill Telemachus. She disguised him as a beggar and he took refuge in a servant's cottage.

Penelope meanwhile could delay no longer. She offered to marry whichever of her suitors could pass the test of stringing Odysseus' bow and shooting an arrow through twelve axe-heads in a row. Of course, all the suitors failed, but Odysseus, still disguised as a beggar, succeeded.

Then he cast off his disguise, revealed himself as King of Ithaca and Penelope's husband. With Telemachus' help, he killed all the suitors.

Heroes and Heroines of Europe

No one knows for sure whether the famous heroes of European literature were purely legendary figures, or whether they were based on people who actually lived. Over the centuries, myths and real events have merged into heroic sagas of dangerous adventures, battles with monsters, dramatic rescues of maidens in distress, and above all, victories of good over evil.

▷ The stories known as the 'Matter of Britain', which were about King Arthur and his knights of the Round Table fellowship, were known and loved all over Europe from about AD 1100 onwards.

These stories were written down in their almost-final version by an English knight called Sir Thomas Mallory around 1470. He called his book *Le Morte d'Arthur*, and this book was one of the first that William Caxton printed when he set up his new fangled printing press in London around 1477.

How Sigurd killed the Dragon

The legend of Sigurd is told in the *Eddas* of Iceland, compiled from storytellers, and also in the *Nibelungenlied*, written by an unknown author in Austria about AD 1200. In this version Sigurd is called Siegfried, and Brynhild becomes Brunhilde.

Sigurd of the Volsungs was one of the greatest heroes of old Norse mythology. The Volsungs were a royal family much favoured by the god Odin, and in fact were said to be descended from him. Sigurd was the son of King Sigmund and Queen Hiordis. When Sigmund died in battle, Hiordis was remarried to Alf, King of the Danes, and the young Sigurd was sent away to be apprenticed to Regin, a famous blacksmith.

As the years passed, Sigurd grew up to be a strong and handsome youth. He learned his trade well and was skilled at his craft. Yet sometimes he was restless and yearned for adventure.

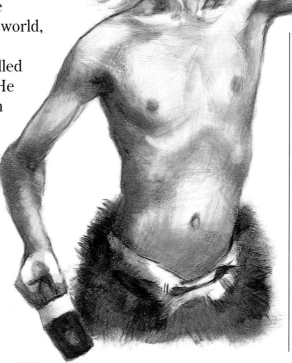

One day, Regin the blacksmith said to Sigurd slyly, 'Always remember that you are the son of Sigmund, and a Volsung, and so are destined for great achievements. I know of a task that only a hero can perform. A while ago, Odin killed my brother, and my father Reidmar demanded compensation. On Odin's behalf, the god Loki obtained a vast hoard of treasure belonging to the Nibelungs who dwell in the underworld, and paid it over as blood money.

'My younger brother, Fafnir, killed my father and stole the treasure. He has changed himself into a dragon and made a lair in which he guards the gold. As the eldest son, that treasure should be mine. You, Sigurd, Prince of the Volsungs, will get it back for me.'

Regin forged for Sigurd a sword so sharp that it could slice through a wisp of wool floating downstream in a river. Armed with this fine sword and mounted on his horse Greyfell, Sigurd set out on his mission.

As Sigurd made his way towards the dragon's lair, an old man appeared from nowhere on the path before him.

When he heard where Sigurd was going, he said, 'No man can approach the dragon face to face without the flames devouring him. Take my advice – dig a pit in the path that Fafnir uses, then hide yourself in it and attack the dragon from below.'

Sigurd thanked him and was about to continue on his way when the old man continued, 'There is one more thing. The dragon's blood has miraculous properties. When you have killed Fafnir, make sure to bathe yourself in his blood and you will become invulnerable to any weapon, disease or fire.' With these words, the stranger vanished. Sigurd realized that he had just met a god.

When Sigurd came to the dragon's track, he followed the old man's advice and dug a deep pit. He waited there, with his sword drawn, and soon felt the ground rumbling and shaking around him. The air grew burning hot with the flames and smoke that engulfed the track, and Sigurd could hear the rattling of scales as the dragon approached. Then its belly slid across the opening of the pit, blocking out the light.

In the darkness, Sigurd thrust his sword upwards with all his strength and felt the blade sink deep into the monster's heart. With a fearsome bellow, Fafnir rolled over on to his side and collapsed.

Blood gushed from the wound and poured down into the pit. Remembering the old man's advice, Sigurd stripped off his clothes and bathed himself in the dragon's blood. But he did not notice that a leaf had fallen on to his shoulder blades as he stooped, and that one place did not receive the magical protection.

When Regin appeared, he ordered Sigurd to roast the dragon's heart, while he himself drank some of the dragon's blood, because he knew that it would enable him to understand the speech of birds and animals.

Sigurd cut out Fafnir's heart and built a fire to roast it on. But he burnt his finger on the roasting heart and licked it, so he, too, tasted the dragon's blood, and gained the power to understand the speech of birds and animals.

Up above, the eagles wheeled and dipped, and now Sigurd could hear what they were saying.

'Sigurd has killed the dragon Fafnir,' they screamed. 'Now the Prince himself will be slain so that Regin alone can keep the Nibelungs' treasure.'

Sigurd turned quickly on Regin and cut the blacksmith to pieces with his

sword before Regin
had time to defend himself.
Then, having also learned that
there was great power in the
heart and blood of Fafnir, Sigurd
ate the meal that he had prepared
for Regin.

After that, Sigurd followed the
dragon's tracks to its lair and found
the treasure in the darkest recesses
of the cave. However, what Sigurd
did not know was that a curse
rested on the treasure of the
Nibelungs, bringing evil and death
to anyone who possessed it.

Sigurd and Brynhild

After killing the dragon Fafnir and winning the treasure of the Nibelungs, Sigurd set off in search of adventure. Riding his horse Greyfell, he visited many faraway lands. He fought for right and won many battles.

Eventually, Sigurd arrived at the court of King Gunther, who ruled over lands beside the River Rhine. Sigurd's noble bearing and tales of his courage won the hearts of the entire court, and in particular of Gunther's sister Kriemhild. Sigurd fell in love with her in return, and asked the King for Kriemhild's hand in marriage. Gunther, however, was more concerned about his own wedding. 'I need your help in wooing the Lady Brynhild,' he confided to Sigurd. 'She lives in a castle surrounded by fire and has vowed never to marry anyone except the hero who dares to ride through the fire to claim her.'

'I will conquer Brynhild for you, if you will let me marry your sister, Kriemhild,' Sigurd vowed.

So Gunther and Sigurd set out for Brynhild's castle. When Gunther saw the raging fire, he was terrified and his horse refused to go forward.

Then Sigurd
took on the shape and face of
Gunther and, thus disguised, rode
through the flames. So he won the hand
of Brynhild and received a ring from her
to prove it. Outside he secretly changed
back to his own shape, and the real Gunther
brought Brynhild back to the Rhine to be his wife.

Sigurd meanwhile was married to Kriemhild. He
gave Brynhild's ring to her and told her the secret of
how he had been the one to win Brynhild for Gunther.

One day, the two queens quarrelled. While they were washing
their hair in the river, Brynhild waded farther out into the current. 'I do
not care to have my hair soiled by water from your hair,' she said to
Kriemhild arrogantly. 'After all, my husband is far superior to yours.'

'My husband is the Prince of the Volsungs,' said Kriemhild proudly.
'He has proved his valour by killing the dragon Fafnir and the scheming
dwarf Regin, as well as by many other great deeds.'

'That's nothing!' retorted Brynhild. 'Only Gunther dared to ride through
the walls of flames to reach me.'

At that, Kriemhild laughed and showed her the ring Brynhild had given
to Sigurd in her own castle. Brynhild realized at once that she had been
won by a trick, and turned pale with anger. She rushed straight to Gunther
and persuaded him that Sigurd must be put to death.

Gunther was reluctant to do this, but he feared Brynhild's wrath, so he
ordered a contest between the strongest warriors of his realm to discover
who was the greatest warrior.

No one could kill Sigurd in open fight, but at last he was murdered by
Gunther's servant Hagen, who had discovered the one place where Sigurd
was vulnerable, between his shoulder blades. He plunged his sword
straight into Sigurd's back, and the Prince of the Volsungs died instantly.

Then, content in the knowledge that the wrong done to her had been
avenged, Brynhild killed herself and was burned on the same funeral pyre.

King Arthur and his Knights

King Arthur is the greatest of the British legendary heroes. Some people believe that he was a real Celtic chieftain, born in the fifth century, who led the Britons in their battles against Saxon invaders. Whether or not this was so, tales of his brave exploits, and those of the knights of his Round Table, were told all over Europe from about AD 1100 onwards.

Arthur was the only son of Uther Pendragon, the King of Britain, by Igraine of Cornwall. As soon as the child was born, the great magician Merlin took him away from his parents to be brought up by a knight called Sir Ector. Merlin's plan was that the future king should grow up not knowing who he was, and should reveal his true identity by a great deed.

In due course, Uther Pendragon died, and because no one knew where Arthur was, the powerful lords began to fight amongst themselves over who should become king. Merlin advised the Archbishop of Canterbury to summon all the lords and knights to London. 'A miracle will reveal the rightful king,' he said.

Sir Ector took the young Arthur and his own son Sir Kay with him to London. On New Year's Day, there was a tournament in which Sir Kay was to take part. After they had left their lodgings, Sir Kay realized that he forgotten his sword, and Arthur went back to fetch it for him. He found the house was locked up, and was wondering what to do when he passed a churchyard. There, in the centre of the churchyard, was a sword stuck into an anvil in the middle of a great marble stone. Inscribed on the sword were these words, 'WHOEVER PULLS THIS SWORD OUT OF THE STONE IS THE RIGHTFUL KING OF ENGLAND.'

Arthur was so pleased to find a sword that he pulled it from the stone without stopping to read the inscription, and rushed off to give it to Sir Kay. But when he told where he had found the sword, nobody believed him.

'Let us return to the churchyard,' suggested Sir Ector, 'so that all the knights can try to pull the sword from the stone.'

Arthur replaced the sword, but none of the knights could move it. Only Arthur was able to draw it free again.

'Arthur, you are the rightful king,' said Sir Kay, and all the other knights knelt down before him and paid him homage.

At Pentecost, Arthur was knighted and crowned King. He set up his court at Camelot, and promised to rule with justice to the end of his days.

△ Merlin was said in legends to be the son of a demon. He was a great wizard, and also had the power of seeing the future. He saved Arthur many times from the attacks of Arthur's half-sister, the wicked enchantress Morgan-le-Fay, who wanted to kill Arthur and give the throne of Britain to one of her own sons.

The Round Table

As part of her dowry, Arthur's wife Guinevere brought to Camelot a fine wooden table. It was so large that 150 knights could sit around it at the same time. Its round shape meant that no knight could lord it over any other, for it had no higher or lower end.

The knights of the Round Table were pledged to serve King Arthur, to fight only for right and always to be merciful and courteous. Every year, at Pentecost, on the anniversary of the day on which Arthur was crowned King, all the knights gathered at Camelot for a feast. They also met at Easter and Christmas. It was the custom that the King did not sit down to eat until he had heard a tale of an heroic adventure or chivalrous deed, or had set before his knights some dangerous new quest.

Sir Gawain and the Green Knight

One Christmas Day, the doors flew open and a huge man rode into Camelot's Great Hall on a great charger. Everything about the stranger was green; he had a green beard and hair, face and hands, and instead of armour, he wore a green cloak. Even his horse was green from head to foot.

The man carried no shield or weapons, except for a huge green axe, and a branch from a holly tree which he held above his head. Flinging the holly branch down on the hall floor, the man looked around at the seated knights.

'I have heard of the bravery and noble deeds of this court,' he cried, 'and I bring a test of valour to your feast. I ask any man here to strike me with this axe, but he must swear to give me the right to do the same to him, twelve months and a day from now. Is any man here courageous enough to exchange stroke for stroke?'

The knights gazed at the huge axe with fear and trepidation. No one dared to answer this fearsome challenge.

The stranger laughed scornfully. 'Can this be the valiant court of King Arthur?' he mocked. 'Are these really the famous knights of the Round Table? Why, they turn pale with fright at the mere mention of a blow!'

At this, King Arthur himself reached out a hand. 'Give me the axe,' he commanded. 'I will strike the blow myself.'

But now Sir Gawain rose to his feet and came forward to the middle of the hall. 'No, uncle,' he said. 'Let this test be mine. I have still to prove my worth as a knight of the Round Table. Let me take up this challenge.'

The stranger leaped from his horse and approached Gawain. 'Tell me your name before we make our bargain,' he said.

'I am Gawain, son of King Lot of Orkney and nephew to King Arthur,' said Gawain. 'I swear that I will strike you one blow with this axe, and that in twelve months and one day I will be prepared to receive a blow from you.'

'Sir Gawain, we will shake on it,' said the Green Knight, clasping Gawain's hand in his own. Then, he knelt down on the floor and bent his head ready for the stroke.

Gawain took up the axe and swung it with all his strength, striking so hard that he chopped off the Green Knight's head and it went rolling across the floor. But the knight did not fall. He simply picked up the severed head and remounted his horse, with the head tucked under his arm.

'I am the Knight of the Green Chapel, and you will find me in the Forest of Wirral in Wales. See to it that you keep your word.' So saying, he turned

and galloped out of the door.

The months passed quickly at Camelot. Each week, knights rode out in search of adventures that would test their knightly skills. Soon the time came for Gawain to set out. Wearing armour inlaid with gold, Gawain mounted his horse Gringalet, and rode off northwards.

Everywhere he went, Gawain asked for news of the Knight of the Green Chapel, but no one had heard of him. At last, exhausted and hungry, Gawain came to a fine castle and decided to ask for food and lodging for the night.

The lord of the castle welcomed Gawain heartily and invited him to stay as long as he wished. Servants led him to a comfortable chamber, where they helped him take off his armour, and dressed him in fine robes. Then they brought silver dishes full of good food and goblets of wine. When Gawain had eaten, he was taken into the main hall and introduced to the lady of the castle, who sang and danced for him.

After a couple of days, Gawain prepared to leave. 'I must continue my search for the Knight of the Green Chapel,' he explained. 'I have sworn to fulfil my quest in three days' time.'

'The Green Chapel is only two hours' ride from here,' said Gawain's host. 'You are welcome to stay here until the day of your quest. I myself will be riding out to hunt, but my wife will entertain you with her company. And to make this a festive occasion, let us agree that I will give you whatever I catch in the forest, and you will give me in exchange anything that comes your way here in the castle.'

'That sounds like a good bargain,' laughed Gawain.

Early next morning, the lord rode off into the forest. Gawain remained in his chamber. Before long the lady of the castle came and sat on his bed, whispering words of love.

'I cannot believe that you are really Sir Gawain,' she said. 'A chivalrous knight would not reject a lady's kisses.' Anxious not to displease his hostess, Gawain accepted a kiss and the lady departed.

When the lord of the castle came home he handed Gawain everything he had caught. 'This is all yours,' he said, 'according to our bargain.'

'And here is everything that I have won within these walls,' said Gawain, giving him a kiss. But he did not tell how he had won it, for that was not part of the bargain.

On the second day, the same thing happened. Gawain received two kisses, which he exchanged for the game caught by the lord of the manor.

On the third day, the lady came again to Gawain's bedchamber and tempted him with words of love and three kisses.

'Please give me something of yours to remember you by,' she begged.

'I have nothing to give you, lady,' said Gawain gravely. 'And I may not give you my love, for you have a husband already.'

'Then take this green lace from me,' said the lady, 'and wear it for my sake. It is magic lace, and while you are wearing it no one can kill you. But make sure you hide it, and don't tell my husband.'

Thinking of his ordeal with the Green Knight the following day, Gawain could not resist taking the gift. That evening, he passed on the three kisses, but said nothing about the lace.

On the morning of the fourth day, Gawain rode out of the castle with a squire to guide him. They came to a valley surrounded by rugged cliffs. There underneath the trees was a low green mound. Gawain sprang from his horse and strode towards it.

'It is I, Gawain of the Round Table,' he called, taking off his helmet and bending his head ready for the blow. 'I have come to keep my bargain.'

The Green Knight came out of the mound with a shining new axe in his hand. Swinging it around, he aimed his blow, but Gawain flinched at the sound of the axe whistling through the air.

'Ha!' cried the Green Knight, lowering the axe. 'Surely you are not frightened of the whistle of the blade? When you struck off my head, I did not flinch even from the blow.'

'I will not flinch again,' promised Gawain. 'But I cannot replace my head as you have yours!'

The Green Knight whirled his axe a second time, and Gawain stood as firm as a rock. But the knight stopped before the blade drew any blood.

'Afraid to strike a defenceless man?' Gawain taunted.

The axe was swung for a third time, but aimed with such care that it merely scraped the skin at the side of Gawain's neck.

However Gawain felt the wound and sprang up. 'That was the blow! If you strike again it is more than our bargain, and I may defend myself.'

'You have indeed fulfilled your oath,' said the Green Knight. 'For my part, I could have struck off your head, had I so wished. I did not touch you on the first stroke, or on the second, because you kept your promise to me and passed on my wife's kisses. The third time, you gave me the three kisses but not the lace. For that I had to wound you.'

'I am ashamed of my cowardice and deceit,' said Gawain, handing him the green lace. 'I am indeed unworthy to be a knight of the Round Table.'

'Come now,' cried the Green Knight. 'You are the bravest and most chivalrous knight in the whole world! Keep the green lace in memory of this adventure and return to Camelot in triumph.'

So the two knights embraced each other, and Gawain rode back to Camelot, where he took his place with renewed honour at the Round Table.

Roland and Oliver

The greatest hero of France was Charlemagne, or Charles I.
Unlike King Arthur, Charlemagne was a real person, King of the
Franks and the Holy Roman Emperor, but tales of his exploits
are mainly legendary. The legends of Charlemagne and his
French knights are told in an epic poem called *La Chanson de
Roland*. The poem is written in the Anglo-Norman dialect, so
may have been composed either in England or northern France.

Charlemagne ruled over a large and powerful Christian
empire. For several years, he had been fighting the
Saracens, the Turkish Moslems who had conquered
Spain. The King's most loyal and courageous knight, and his
right-hand man in battle, was his nephew, Roland.

Marsilius was one of the Christian kings of Spain who had surrendered
to the Moslem Turks. He had been defeated so many times by the Saracens
that in desperation he agreed to help them against Charlemagne.

When the French army marched into the territory of Marsilius and
ordered him to submit to Charlemagne, Marsilius begged for peace and
said he would pay tribute in gold and silver. He asked Charlemagne to send
an intermediary to arrange the terms.

Charlemagne pondered over whom he should send to talk to Marsilius.
Should it be the brave and faithful Roland, the Champion of France, or the
crafty Ganelon, who was also Roland's stepfather? He chose Ganelon,
warning him to be on his guard against Marsilius' treachery.

Ganelon travelled to Saragossa and was received with great honour by
Marsilius. After several days of feasts and tournaments, Marsilius invited
Ganelon to walk with him in the palace gardens.

'Your ruler, Charlemagne, has done me great harm,' Marsilius said. 'He
has invaded my land and brought great suffering to my people.'

Surprised to hear Marsilius speak ill of Charlemagne in this way,
Ganelon replied that Charlemagne had marched into Spain to fight the
Saracens, the enemy of Christians. 'It is you, Marsilius, who has given
support to these non-believers,' Ganelon pointed out.

'I hear that Charlemagne plans to give Roland lands and castles in Spain
as a reward for his services,' said Marsilius craftily.

Ganelon scowled, for he was jealous of the regard and affection that
Charlemagne showed to his stepson.

'If Roland was killed, surely you would take his place in Charlemagne's
favour?' Marsilius continued.

Ganelon was easily won over, and the two men drew up a plan. Roland
would be invited to come to the village of Roncesvalles, which lay between

the two armies, to receive the tribute. But instead of silver and gold, he would find the whole of Marsilius' army waiting for him.

While the traitor Ganelon took refuge in France, Roland set off for Spain with a band of one hundred knights, including his friend Oliver.

When they reached the village of Roncesvalles, Roland sent Oliver to look out from the mountain top. Oliver soon came thundering back down the slope, angry and dismayed. 'A whole army is encamped in the valley dressed in full battle armour,' he cried. 'They have not come for peace.'

'I should have suspected it,' said Roland grimly. 'But our duty now is to find Marsilius and kill him as an enemy. Remember that every man here is a true knight and must stand and fight as a champion of Charlemagne. The blood that will be shed here today will be remembered for ever.'

The little band of knights took their places in the pass and the first charge against them crumbled as they stood firm as a rock. Spanish horses wheeled away out of the battle, their riders hanging lifeless from the saddles. Of the French knights, only Oliver was wounded, but he remained in his saddle, waiting for the next attack.

Then a second army, this time of Saracens, came into view. They were armed with scimitars, the two-edged swords feared by the Christians. The leader of the Saracen army, King Falseron, rode out ahead of his army.

'Roland!' he yelled. 'My son died in battle by your hand. Now I come to avenge his death!' And so saying, he charged at the French knight.

But Roland was too quick for him, and thrust his lance through Falseron's body before he could lift his shield. As Falseron fell lifeless from his horse, a groan went up from the Saracen army. They would have left the battlefield immediately, but Marsilius cut off their retreat with his own men.

The battle raged fiercely. Twenty of Marsilius' men fell for every one of the French knights, but Roland grieved to see his men go down under the hooves of the enemy cavalry.

Oliver bravely killed Saracens with his lance and sword until an arrow pierced his armour and he, too, fell down dead.

At last, surrounded by only a handful of knights, Roland raised his great horn Olifant, carved from an ivory tusk to his lips and blew three times.

Thirty miles away, Charlemagne heard the notes of the horn roll through the mountains and knew it was the sound of a man desperate for help. But even as the French army began to move towards Roncesvalles, Roland was nearing the end of his long battle. His horse grew weary first, buckled at the knees, and rolled over dead. Then Roland, overcome by his wounds, sank to the ground and died.

By the time Charlemagne reached the battlefield, it was all over. The heroic band of knights were all dead, but as Roland had prophesied, their bravery was remembered for ever.

Lady Bradamante, Knight of France

Between 1480 and 1530, two Italian poets were writing at the court of Ferrara in Italy. Mateo Boiardo, in his *Orlando Innamorato*, and Ludovico Ariosto, in his *Orlando Furioso*, retold the legends of Charlemagne and his knights, including many new adventures.

One of the famous legendary heroines of Charlemagne's reign was a young female knight called Bradamante, who rode into battle wearing a white plume in her helmet and carrying a white shield. Bradamante's prowess in battle was so great that few of the other knights realized she was a woman. During her travels, Bradamante met and fell in love with a Saracen knight called Rogero. After they were parted in a battle, she set out to look for her lover.

Bradamante made her way through a forest in search of Rogero, and came to a beautiful fountain whose waters flowed through a broad meadow. Many travellers had stopped to rest and refresh themselves in the shade of the trees that grew beside the quiet waters. Among the travellers was a knight who appeared to be in great distress. He told Bradamante that his name was Pinabel, and that his sweetheart had been taken from him by a magician who descended from the skies on a winged horse.

'I chased after them until my horse was no longer able to carry me,' he told her, 'and two other knights also pursued the enchanter on my behalf. Now they are prisoners in his castle on top of the mountain. Their names are Gradasso, King of Sericane, and Rogero the Saracen.'

Bradamante's heart leapt at the mention of Rogero's name. 'Sir Knight,' she said. 'Do not despair. Lead me to the castle where they are held.'

As they made their way towards the castle, the two knights were overtaken by a messenger who had been sent to summon Bradamante back to camp. In this way, Pinabel learned that she was a member of the Clermont family, with whom his own family waged an ancient feud. From this moment, he resolved to get rid of his companion as quickly as possible.

Bradamante decided to ignore the summons, and, with Pinabel leading the way, they arrived at the foot of a steep, rocky mountain. They climbed up until they came to the mouth of a cavern.

Pinabel, seeing a way of ridding himself of Bradamante, exclaimed that he could see that a young girl was trapped far down below.

Without a moment's hesitation, Bradamante lopped off a branch of a nearby elm tree with her sword and told Pinabel to hold it while she lowered herself down into the abyss. When she was halfway down, the scheming traitor let go of the branch so that Bradamante fell.

Fortunately, the twigs and foliage broke her descent so that, although stunned by the fall, the brave young knight was uninjured.

As soon as she had recovered from the shock, Bradamante looked around her and saw she was in a subterranean temple with columns and walls of pure alabaster.

A priestess dressed in a flowing robe came forward to welcome her, saying, 'Brave and noble Bradamante, a divine power has brought you to this grotto so that you may be warned of the dangers that await you. The magician who holds Rogero captive wears on his arm a shield that flashes a brilliant light. It is so bright that anyone who looks at it is blinded. It is no use shutting your eyes, because then you will not be able to see to fight him. However, I will tell you what you must do.

'Agramant, the Saracen Prince, is also anxious to have Rogero back, and has sent his servant Brunello to snatch him from the demon. Brunello is wearing a magic ring that has the power to break all spells.

'Follow Brunello to the castle and take the ring from him, but be careful. If he puts the ring into his mouth, he can make himself invisible and so you will lose him.'

The next morning, Bradamante set off on her quest and soon met up with Brunello. Just then the sky turned dark as a huge winged horse flew overhead. Like a griffin, it had the head of an eagle, huge claws and feathered wings. On its back was mounted a cavalier in shining armour.

'That is the enchanter who lives on top of the mountain,' said Brunello. 'Many knights have gone to attack him, but none have ever returned.'

'I plan to try myself,' said Bradamante. 'May I follow you?'

So Bradamante followed Brunello until they came to a rugged, perpendicular rock. Looking upwards, they saw a castle perched high on the summit, surrounded by a wall made of brass. Catching him unaware, Bradamante seized Brunello and bound him to a tree, taking the magic ring from his finger and placing it on her own. Then she advanced to the foot of the rock and blew her horn. The enchanter appeared almost immediately. He carried no weapons and in his hand there was an open book.

Bradamante attacked the enchanter fiercely, striking at him again and again with her sword, but could not wound him. When she saw that he was preparing to uncover the shield that he wore on his arm, she threw herself to the ground. As the enchanter approached, she sprang up and seized him.

'Tell me who you are, and why you have built this fortress,' she demanded, holding him fast.

'It is not for any evil purpose,' replied the enchanter. 'It was only to guard the life of a young knight called Rogero. I have raised him since childhood, but he left me to follow the Saracen Prince, Agramant, in his invasion of France. I have brought him here in the hope of saving him from war. I have collected a number of knights and ladies in my castle to provide Rogero with company and entertainment. Take as many of them as you like, but spare my beloved Rogero. I assure you he lives in luxury and has many pleasures and companions.'

'But he does not have his liberty,' cried Bradamante, 'which is all that a true knight desires.' She lost no time in setting Rogero free, along with all the other captives.

Bradamante and Rogero descended from the mountain and found the winged horse waiting for them, with the magic shield tied to its saddle. The fearless Rogero sprang on to its back, but when the animal felt his spurs it spread its wings and soared into the air.

Bradamante saw her lover snatched away again, as the horse carried Rogero off over the tops of the mountains. However, after many more adventures, the lovers were eventually reunited and married.

Cu Chulainn, the Hound of Ulster

Cu Chulainn was brought up by four wise men, and when they offered him the choice of a long life or fame, Cu Chulainn chose fame. Among the taboos that the wise men laid down for Cu Chulainn were that he was never to pass a hearth without tasting the food being cooked there, and he must never eat the flesh of a dog. They also predicted that Cu Chulainn would be a mighty warrior, and that his first and last exploits would be killing a dog.

In fact, he got his name, which means 'Hound of Ulster', at the age of seven, when he killed a huge watchdog belonging to Culann the smith by picking it up by the legs and dashing it to pieces against a stone.

By the age of twelve, Cu Chulainn was a formidable warrior. Armed with his special weapon, the 'gae bolga', he did battle with human enemies, supernatural beings and monsters.

The fame promised by the wise men first came to him when he was challenged by the three giant sons of Nechtar, who were deadly enemies of Conchobar of Ulster. The first son Cu Chulainn killed by hurling an iron ball at his head. He pierced the second son through the heart with a mighty thrust of his sword. Cu Chulainn wrestled with the third son in a river ford, eventually overpowering him and striking off his head.

Cu Chulainn set off for home carrying their three severed heads. On the way, the young warrior proved his power over animals as well as over men. He caught a stag by subduing it with the power of his eyes, and then shot at some swans flying overhead with his slingshot, but brought them down alive.

Cu Chulainn was a handsome young man, and with his gift for poetry was very popular in court circles, particularly with the women. When he carried off Emer as his wife, her father Forgall plotted his death. But Cu Chulainn stormed Forgall's fortress and pursued him to his death off the ramparts.

Cu Chulainn had a son, Conlai, by another woman. Conlai, who was brought up in his mother's country, swore never to reveal his identity and never to decline a fight. When he came to Ulster, he was challenged to identify himself and defeated two of Conchobar's best warriors. Cu Chulainn had to defend the honour of Ulster against his own son, and fought and killed him.

The warrior hero won many battles and had many adventures, but he came to his own death in the way that

▽ One of the most famous Irish folk heroes was Cu Chulainn. According to tradition, he was the son of the god Lug and nephew of the great chieftain Conchobar.

The early Irish stories known as the *Ulster Cycle* are thought to be based on historical fact. Passed on by word of mouth long before they were written down, most of them are about the warrior heroes who followed Conchobar of Ulster. He is said to have ruled at the beginning of the Christian era about 2,000 years ago.

had been predicted. On the way to his last battle, Cu Chulainn passed a fire where three sorceresses were roasting a dog. He hesitated, not sure what to do, and then decided to eat a joint of the meat. He used his left hand to hold the meat, and this hand subsequently lost its strength.

As a result, his enemies were able to give him a mortal wound, but Cu Chulainn tied himself to a stone pillar so that he would die on his feet, rather than lying ignominiously on the ground.

The Arabian Nights

The *Arabian Nights* is a collection of ancient stories from the Arab world about the adventures of heroes, merchants, sultans, caliphs, princes and princesses, strange beasts and genies. The Arab people were firm believers in the influence of good and evil spirits on the human race. The powers of these spirits could be invoked by magic talismans, such as the famous lamp which Aladdin used to call up the genie.

SCHEHERAZADE

The stories of the *Arabian Nights* are narrated by Scheherazade, wife of King Schahriar. This King had once been married to a very beautiful woman who deceived him with a handsome slave from his guard.

To make sure that no woman could deceive him again, he swore that he would marry a new wife each day, and that each new wife would be executed on the morning after their wedding. This went on until Scheherazade, the daughter of his vizier, became his wife.

Just before the time fixed for her execution, Scheherazade began telling the King a fascinating story, and he spared her life for another night because he badly wanted to hear the end. However, as soon as Scheherazade had finished the first story, she cleverly began another leading out of it, to keep the King's interest involved. She continued in this way for a thousand and one nights, by which time Schahriar was so in love with her, and so convinced of her faithfulness, that she remained his queen for ever.

▷▷ Scheherazade is typical of the women that she describes in her many stories. She is educated, well read, worldly and intelligent.

The women in her stories often organize their own lives, run their own households, take revenge on unfaithful lovers, and are usually more prudent and forethoughtful than the men who frequently bring serious trouble on themselves by their curiosity or rashness.

THE CALIPH'S GLASSES

One of her stories tells what happened to Caliph Haroun al Rashid of Baghdad when he wandered in disguise among his people, putting wrongs right and punishing the guilty. An old craftsman had a son who was about to be sentenced for committing a serious offence. The craftsman begged the Caliph for mercy, and Rashid said he would pardon the young man if his father could invent some device for detecting an honest man.

The craftsman made a pair of spectacles of very thick glass with thin golden frames. When the Caliph put them on and looked at the eminent citizens of Baghdad who had gathered to watch the demonstration, he could see none of their faces. The only person he could see was a servant, standing at the back. Concluding that this was the only honest man among his followers, Rashid promoted the young man to high office.

However, a few months later, the Caliph found that he could no longer see the young man's face through the glasses. And so he decided that it must be impossible for any man to hold high office and still remain honest. The Caliph therefore destroyed the glasses because he knew they would prevent him from trusting anyone ever again.

FLYING CARPETS

A prince called Hussain once bought a flying carpet in order to try and win the hand of his lovely cousin.

Hussain and his two brothers were all in love with Nouronnihar and wanted to marry her. Their father, the sultan, ordered that the brothers should travel for a while, and the one who brought back the most remarkable object would marry her.

Ali found an ivory tube through which one could see anything in the world – and saw that Nouronnihar was about to die from a dreadful disease. Ahmed found an apple which could cure any disease.

The three brothers flew to their cousin's bedside on Hussain's flying carpet. With the help of the magic apple, Nouronnihar was cured. But the sultan could not decide which was the most remarkable object, and ordered an archery contest to settle the matter. Prince Ahmed won the match, while Hussain then met and married a peri (a fairy).

△ Flying carpets are made in the city of Bisnagar in India. They are a popular method of transport in the *Arabian Nights*, carrying up to three passengers to any destination.

Sinbad the Sailor

Long ago, in Baghdad, there lived a poor man called Sinbad who earned his living as a porter. One day, he sat down to rest outside the house of a rich man whose name was also Sinbad. Struck by the difference between their two lives, 'Why am I so poor, and he so rich?' he cried aloud. Hearing these words, the rich man invited the porter to his table, and told him the following tale.

'When I was still young, my father died, leaving me a large fortune. I spent most of my wealth until I realized that I had better try to make some more money with the little I had left. So I bought some goods and set sail for the Persian Gulf, hoping to sell at a profit.

'The ship called at several places and we did some trading, and then one day I was accidentally marooned on an island, where I became friendly with the chief and some of the natives. I exchanged my goods for articles made only on the island, which I later sold for a large sum of money. I had no further need to work, but I soon tired of doing nothing and set sail again.

'On the second voyage, we reached what seemed to be a desert island. I climbed a tree to get my bearings, and saw something smooth and white, as big as a dome. While I was wondering what it was, the sky darkened and a gigantic bird flew down and settled on the dome. It was a rukh's egg, and the rukh spread herself over the egg to brood. I crept under the bird and lashed myself to one of her legs with my turban.

'When the rukh flew off in the morning, she carried me with her to a deep valley, where the ground was covered with diamonds. I untied myself from her leg, and bent down to gather a handful. But then I saw a writhing mass of huge black snakes, and fled to the safety of a cave.

'After a while, I heard something fall with a heavy thud, and saw a large piece of raw meat lying close to my feet. Another piece fell, and another. As they fell on the diamonds, the stones stuck firmly into the meat. Then I remembered the sailors' stories, and knew that the meat was being thrown into the valley by men high up on the mountains, in the hope that eagles would carry it up to feed their young ones, bringing the diamonds with it.

'Now I saw a way of escape. I tied a piece of meat firmly to my back, and waited for an eagle to carry me up out of the valley. But first, I filled my pockets with diamonds, so that when I reached home again I was able to settle down to a comfortable life.

'However a longing for travel soon came over me, and I set off on a third voyage. This time, a strong wind blew our ship towards a rocky island. As we dropped anchor, a horde of hideous apes with yellow eyes and black faces swarmed on to the ship and dragged us ashore. At sunset, a gigantic ape, as tall as a palm tree and black as coal, emerged from his fortress. The monster seized one of the sailors and devoured him for supper. This went on for several evenings until those of us who still survived made rafts from the wreckage along the shore and found a way into the fortress.

'We put out the monster's eyes as he was sleeping, but he had a mate, and they both came after us as we ran for the rafts. The monster's mate bombarded us with boulders and sank all the rafts except the one on which I stood. I managed to paddle out of range and was rescued by a passing ship.

'On the fourth voyage my friends were eaten by cannibals and I

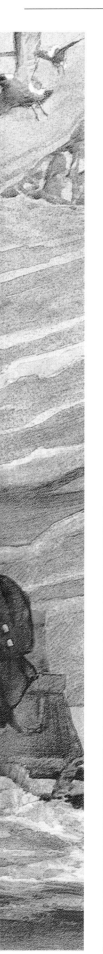

was buried alive. But when I finally arrived back, the pleasures of being home soon made me forget past dangers, and so it was not long before I set sail once again.

'On my fifth voyage, two gigantic rukhs bombarded our ship with huge boulders. A direct hit sank the ship and everyone perished except me. I floated off on some wreckage and landed on the shore of a pleasant island, where there was plenty of fruit and fresh water to drink. By a brook, I saw a little old man, who wanted me to carry him across on my back. But when I tried to put him down on the other side, he twisted his legs tightly around my waist and his arms around my neck and clung to me, nonstop day and night.

'At last, I came to the spot where, a few days before, I had left the juice of some grapes in an empty gourd. The juice had fermented in the sun and turned into wine. The old man asked for a drink, and the wine made him so drowsy that his grip slackened and I was able to throw him off my back and kill him with a big stone.

'Then I met some sailors who had put into the island to gather coconuts. The trees were so tall that I wondered how we would get the nuts, but the sailors threw stones at some monkeys, and they in return pelted us with coconuts. We did this each day until we had enough coconuts to fill the whole ship. I exchanged my coconuts for pearls and spices in the places that we called at on the return voyage.

'You will perhaps be wondering why, after so many dangers, I set off on a sixth voyage, when I could have stayed quietly at home. I wonder myself now, but at the time I was eager to set out again. After many days at sea, the ship was wrecked on a rocky shore. There seemed to be no hope of escape, for the shore was covered with wrecks and the bones of those who had died there. The most careful ate only a little of their food each day, so they lived longer than others. At last I was the only one left.

'Then an idea came into my head. I made a raft with the pieces of timber on the shore, loaded it with goods, and stepped aboard. I guided the raft away from the rocks with an oar, and hoped that the currents would carry me to some other island. Several days passed, and I fell into an exhausted slumber. I awoke to find myself surrounded by a group of dark-skinned men, and told them of my adventures.

'They took me at once to their king who treated me with great kindness. I stayed there for several months, but though the time passed pleasantly enough, I longed to return home. The King of the Indies agreed to this at once, and gave me many valuable gifts to take to the Caliph.

'I thought that this was the end of my travels, but one day the Caliph summoned me to the palace and asked me to take gifts from him to the King of the Indies. On the way back, the ship was seized by pirates and I was taken and sold as a slave.

'My master took me with him to shoot elephants, in order to get the ivory from their tusks. Every day, we shot an elephant, until one great animal tore up the tree in which I was hiding and carried me to a valley filled with the bones of dead elephants. He seemed to know it was only their tusks that I wanted, and so he brought me to their burying place. My master's storehouses were soon full of tusks. He set me free, giving me a ship to sail home in and filling it with ivory.

'My family and friends welcomed me joyfully, and since my last voyage I have lived a quiet life, doing good whenever possible.'

Sinbad the Sailor turned to the porter and said, 'Now that you have heard my tale, I think you will agree that I have earned the riches I enjoy?'

Sinbad the Porter rose and kissed his host's hand. 'I see now that your troubles have been much greater than mine,' he said. 'You deserve everything you have, and I hope you will live a long and happy life.'

The Enchanted Horse

The Shah of Persia and his entourage were celebrating the New Year festival when an unknown Indian man appeared at court, leading a magnificent horse. Everyone gathered around to admire the splendid beast, but when they looked more closely discovered that it was not a real horse at all. To their astonishment, the Indian mounted the horse and turned a small peg in its neck to make it fly.

The Shah was very impressed by this amazing invention, and the Indian offered to give him the horse in exchange for his daughter. The Shah suggested that his son, Prince Firouz, should try the horse first.

Firouz mounted the horse, and without waiting for any instructions turned the peg and flew away. The Indian was alarmed when the horse vanished from sight, and begged the Shah not to be angry with him if Firouz came to any harm. But the Shah put the man in prison and said he would be executed if the prince did not return within three months.

The enchanted horse carried Firouz high over the mountains of the Himalayas and the plains of India until eventually he landed on the roof of a palace, the home of the Princess of Bengal. Prince Firouz fell instantly in love with her and brought the Princess back to Persia as his bride.

The Indian was released from prison when Firouz and his bride returned, but he was angry at the way he had been treated, so he abducted the Princess on his enchanted horse. Landing in a remote valley in Kashmir, he tried to force his attentions on her.

The Princess's cries for help were heard by the Sultan of Kashmir, who imprisoned the Indian and determined to marry the Princess himself. She didn't want to marry the Sultan at all, and so she pretended to be mad.

In the meantime, Prince Firouz had been searching for his bride. Hearing the tales of the mad Princess, he disguised himself as a physician and went to rescue her. He explained to the Sultan that the Princess was not mad, but merely enchanted. She had arrived on an enchanted horse and could only be cured by mounting the horse again and breathing in the smoke of magical perfumes.

The Sultan agreed to this plan and ordered fires to be lit. Prince Firouz sprinkled various powders into the flames and, under cover of the thick smoke screen, took off on the enchanted horse with the Princess behind him. Before the Sultan realized what had happened, they were far away.

After a peaceful flight, the Prince and Princess landed safely in Baghdad and on the very next day they were married under the delighted eyes of the Shah of Persia.

As for the scheming Indian, he was beheaded after all by the furious Sultan of Kashmir.

◁ Mechanical devices are a particular feature of the stories of the *Arabian Nights*. They are far more common in these stories than in tales from Europe, where wizards and magicians usually employ spirits to carry out their spells.

The enchanted horse is by no means the most extraordinary machine described in Scheherazade's epic story-telling session.

Heroes and Heroines of Asia

The two great mythological epics of India are the *Mahabharata* and the *Ramayana*. In these stories, the heroes are considered to be gods who have been reborn on Earth. Their descents to Earth are called 'avatars'.

In the *Mahabharata*, probably composed in its present 18-book form about 300 BC, the heroes are the Pandava brothers, the five sons of Kunti and various gods. They are helped in their struggle against their evil cousins by the god Krishna.

In early versions of the *Ramayana*, the hero Rama is human, but later he is spoken of as a god, an incarnation on Earth of the great god Vishnu. It was also written down about 300 BC.

▽ The *Mahabharata* in its final 18-book form, is longer than the *Iliad* and the *Odyssey* combined.
The *Ramayana* is not quite as long, but still runs to over 100,000 lines of poetry.

Kunti calls on the Gods

Kunti was the daughter of a nymph and a Brahmin. When she was still a girl, the sage Dhurvasa taught Kunti a prayer charm, or mantra. 'By the power of this mantra,' Dhurvasa said, 'you can call upon any of the gods to do your bidding, and you will become the mother of their sons.'

One day, Kunti watched the sun god Surya passing across the sky and wondered whether, if she uttered the mantra, he would really come to her side. No sooner had she spoken it than the god descended from heaven in his golden chariot. When he returned to his kingdom in the sky, Kunti became the mother of his son, who was called Karna. The child was born wearing shining golden armour and earrings that glowed with a reddish light.

Kunti was frightened of what she had done, so she sadly put the baby Karna in a basket and floated it down the river. He was found by a peasant couple who lived on the river bank and brought up as their own son.

Meanwhile, Kunti was given in marriage to King Pandu, who also took a second wife called Madri. The two wives got on well together and they all lived happily until King Pandu, while out hunting, killed a god in the form of a deer. The dying deer put a curse on Pandu that he would never have children because if he lay with his wives, he would die.

Pandu was so heartbroken at the thought of having no son and heir, that Kunti told him about the mantra she had been taught by the sage Dhurvasa.

When he had listened to her story, Pandu said, 'The gods have blessed you in this way so that you can fulfil a divine purpose. Pray first to Dharma, the son of Brahma and god of justice. The son born to him will lead our people on the right path.'

So Kunti prayed to Dharma, and so the noble prince Yudhishthira was born.

Then Pandu urged his wife to pray for a second son by the wind god Vayu. This child was named Bhima – he was so strong that he caused a minor earthquake when he was born. By Indra, the storm king, Kunti gave birth to the brave warrior Arjuna.

When Arjuna drove out at the start of the great battle, he was so horrified at the prospect of the slaughter ahead that he hesitated to start the battle. His cousin, the god Krishna, was driving his chariot – the dialogue between the cousins, known as the *Bhagavad Gita*, is one of the most famous sections of the whole poem.

After this, Kunti declined to have any more children, although Pandu was eager for more. So Kunti taught Madri the mantra, and she prayed to the Aswins, the twin gods of the dawn, and bore twin sons, Nakula and Sahadeva. The five brothers became known as the Pandavas.

However Pandu did not live to see his sons grow to manhood. One day, he died suddenly, and Madri was so upset that she threw herself on to Pandu's funeral pyre.

Kunti took the fatherless boys to live with Pandu's blind brother, Dhritarashtra, who became king after Pandu. He brought them up with his own hundred sons, who were known as the Kauravas. Dhritarashtra was kind to Pandu's boys, but his sons were jealous of their cousins, particularly after Yudhishthira was formally named heir to the throne.

As the young men grew up, their rivalry became greater. At first, they challenged each other in tournaments and contests, but in the end there was a great battle that lasted for eighteen days. The Pandavas finally defeated the Kauravas, killing them all. Yudhishthira took his rightful place on the throne, and became a great king who ruled for many years.

How Rama rescued Sita

Along time ago, Dasa Ratha was ruler of a kingdom in India. He had four fine grown-up sons, of whom Rama, the eldest, was the strongest and most handsome. Rama was the best shot with a bow and arrow, the best rider on horseback, and the most valiant of the princes in battle.

The King also had three wives, as was the custom in India in those days. The youngest wife, Kaikeyi, was jealous of Rama and wanted her son to be heir. So she persuaded Dasa Ratha to banish Rama from the kingdom for fourteen years.

Rama dressed as a poor man and went to live in the jungle, taking with him his beautiful wife Sita and his younger brother Lakshman. The three of them lived happily enough in a bamboo hut, eating berries and wild fruits and making friends with the animals. Holy men visited them in their exile, and one gave Rama a bow with a quiver of magic arrows.

One day, Ravana, the Demon King, saw Sita gathering berries and fell in love with her. He sent evil spirits to capture Sita, but Rama fought them off with his magic arrows. Then, Ravana sent one of his demons disguised as a deer, and as soon as Sita saw the pretty little animal, she begged Rama to catch it for her.

Rama gathered up his bow and followed the deer. After a time, Sita and Lakshman heard a cry of pain, and Rama's voice called from the trees, 'Lakshman! Help me! I am being attacked by a demon.'

Telling Sita not to leave the hut, Lakshman went to his brother's aid. But while he was away, Ravana lured Sita out of the hut by pretending to be an old beggar. To Sita's horror, the beggar turned into the Demon King, and ten heads grew out of his body. Ravana then carried Sita away in his chariot.

When Rama and Lakshman returned, they found that Sita had gone. Hanuman, king of the monkeys, promised to help in the search. After many weeks, Hanuman arrived at the very edge of India by the sparkling blue sea, and a bird told him that a chariot with a weeping woman in it had flown

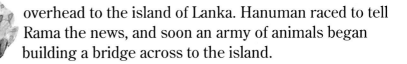

overhead to the island of Lanka. Hanuman raced to tell Rama the news, and soon an army of animals began building a bridge across to the island.

Hanuman went ahead, but he was caught by Ravana and, as a cruel punishment, an oil-soaked rag was tied to his tail and set alight. Hanuman danced in pain across the rooftops, setting fire to the houses as he went, so that flames and smoke rose from the burning city. Hanuman was in such pain that he put his tail in his mouth and the flame went out, but the inside of his mouth turned black, which is why to this day monkeys have black roofs to their mouths.

Meanwhile Rama gathered together an army of animals and sent his most fearsome monkey warrior Angada with a message to the Demon King, 'Despicable Ravana, in my absence you have carried away the helpless Sita. Restore her at once or you will be punished for your wicked crime.'

When Ravana heard Rama's message his eyes grew red with anger. 'Seize the messenger and kill him!' he shouted.

Four huge Rakshasas grabbed hold of Angada, but the monkey wrapped his huge arms around them and holding them fast leapt up to the ramparts. Raising the Rakshasas high above his head, he hurled them down to the ground, crushing their skulls and bones. Then with a mighty kick he broke off a turret of the Demon King's palace. After this revenge, he returned to Rama and reported what had happened.

Rama immediately ordered his army to attack, and with shouts of 'Victory to Rama!' the animals rushed on the city. Ravana's army was already there to meet them, and they fought a long and bitter battle.

The Rakshasas were armed with bows, axes, spears and swords. The monkey warriors threw boulders and trees, and used their nails and fists. Thousands died on both sides, and soon the battlefield was covered with corpses and rivers of blood.

For the whole day the battle raged. Ravana's son Indrajit, finding his horses and charioteer slain and the chariot smashed by Angada, decided to use sorcery. Fixing into his bow some special darts that had the power to bind a victim and make him helpless and unable to move, he shot them at Rama and Lakshman. The brothers tottered and fell. Indrajit proudly reported to his father that they lay senseless on the battlefield.

Ravana embraced his victorious son and sent a message to Sita. 'Go and tell Sita that her husband has been slain by Indrajit's darts, and that Lakshman, too, lies dead on the battlefield,' he commanded.

When Sita heard this message, she wept and wailed and joined her hands in prayer for her beloved husband. The monkey warriors mourned the loss of their leader. But as time passed, and the strength of the sorcery lessened, the brothers woke up from their magical trance and prepared once more for battle.

Rama's magic bow and arrows killed many of Ravana's champions, and then an arrow pierced the Demon King's chest. When the wounded King of the Rakshasas got up, Rama said to him, 'You have fought well today. I will not strike or slay you just now, as you are tired and wounded. Go away and rest for the night. Come back tomorrow, refreshed and fully armed.'

Ravana brooded over his humiliation at the hands of a mere mortal and decided to call on his giant brother Kumbhakarna to help him in the battle on the next morning.

The earth shook as this terrible giant marched out on to the battlefield with a huge spear in his hand. He trampled fifty monkeys under each of his big feet before Rama's magic arrows killed him.

The Demon King, his wound healed, then challenged Rama to a duel. Ravana flung javelins and poison darts at Rama, but they were all deflected by Rama's shield. Then, Rama fired one of the poison darts back with his magic bow and it struck the Demon King and killed him.

By now, fourteen years had passed, and so the victorious hero Rama returned to his own city with his beloved Sita and Lakshman. And all the people turned out to welcome Rama as their rightful prince.

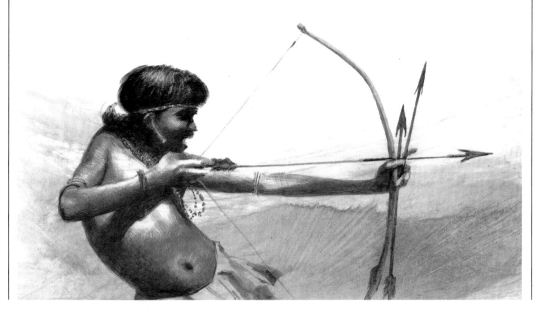

◁ Following Rama's victory, the dead Dasa Ratha appeared and blessed his sons, telling Rama to return and take up his reign. Rama went on to reign righteously for a thousand years.

Heroes and Heroines of Persia

As in many other countries, the legends of ancient Persia (Iran) were handed on by word of mouth long before they were written down. Court minstrels recited poems that glorified the deeds of great warriors and heroes. In time, the exploits of heroes such as Rustam and Ardashir were recorded in the great national epic of Iran, the *Shah-nama*, first written down about AD 1020.

Rustam and Sohrab, his Son

The great warrior Rustam was such a strong baby that ten foster mothers were needed to nurse him. By the time he was weaned, he ate enough for five children.

One day, when Rustam was still a child, the King's white elephant ran amok, killing several men. The sleeping Rustam was woken by the shouting. Grasping his father's mace, he knocked off the head of a guard who tried to block his way and ran out to confront the beast. It was raging like the Nile in flood, but Rustam attacked fearlessly and killed it with one blow of the mace.

When he grew up, Rustam travelled around Iran on his famous horse Rakhsh. Among his numerous heroic feats, he overcame a ferocious lion, fought a dragon, and killed a sorceress and a great white demon.

After one such exploit, Rustam lay down to rest while Rakhsh roamed about the plain grazing. A group of horsemen passed by, caught Rakhsh with a lasso and carried him off. When Rustam woke and found that his horse was missing, he made his way on foot to the palace at Samangan.

'Rakhsh is too well known to be hidden for long,' said the King reassuringly. 'Meantime, you are welcome to stay here.'

A great feast was prepared, and afterwards Rustam was shown into a fine bedchamber and fell into a deep sleep. During the night, the King's daughter Tahmina came to Rustam and begged him to lie with her, saying that she wanted a son who would match Rustam in strength and manly qualities. A priest was called and they were married.

Rustam gave his bride the jewelled amulet that he wore on his arm. 'Look after this,' he said. 'If you should give birth to a daughter, tie it to her hair to bring good fortune. If the gods send you a son, bind it to his arm in token of his father.'

Next morning, the King gave Rustam the good news that Rakhsh had been discovered. Rustam went to the place where the horse was stabled and caressed him, put on a saddle and, with the speed of wind, left Samangan to go back to Iran, telling no one what had happened to him.

A son was born to princess Tahmina, and he was given the name of Sohrab. At one month old, it was as if the child had reached twelve months, and by the age of three, he was already training for the battlefield. By his fifth year, Sohrab had the courage of a lion, and by the time he reached his tenth year, no man in Samangan would dare to challenge him in combat.

One day, Sohrab said to his mother, 'Tell me, since I am much taller and stronger than all my cousins here, who is my father?'

To this his mother replied, 'Now that you are fully grown you have a right to know. You are the son of Rustam, the greatest warrior who ever lived.'

Tahmina showed Sohrab a letter from Rustam, which he had sent from Iran when his son was born, with three rubies and three purses of gold.

'Why have you kept this a secret from me?' demanded Sohrab. 'I am proud to have such ancestry, for everyone talks about Rustam's heroic deeds.'

'If your father were to know how strong and handsome you have grown, he would summon you to go to him, and that would break my heart,' Tahmina replied.

'Now you will see some heroic deeds from me,' said Sohrab firmly. 'I will raise some men and march against Iran. I will bestow the treasury and the crown on my father Rustam, and put him in place of Shah Kavus. And you will be his queen.'

Then Sohrab gathered some troops and asked his grandfather for supplies and permission to depart. News of the impending attack reached Kavus, who prepared his men to fight. Before the battle, Sohrab captured one of the Iranian knights and asked him to point out Rustam to him. The Iranian, overawed by Sohrab's strength, was afraid that Rustam would be killed by Sohrab, so he told Sohrab that Rustam was not present in the Iranian camp.

Rustam mounted his horse Rakhsh and prepared for combat. When he caught sight of Sohrab, he was amazed at the young warrior's towering strength, and judged him a worthy rival. 'Let us fight man to man, as one warrior to another,' he suggested to Sohrab.

And so it came about that Rustam and Sohrab faced each other on the battlefield. At first, the two men wielded short lances. Soon, these were destroyed, and they exchanged blows with swords, until these too broke into pieces. Then, they pounded each other with heavy spears, which bent under the weight of their blows. Armour came clattering down off the horses, and chain mail dropped in fragments between the two warriors.

In time, both men and horses were exhausted. Their bodies ran with sweat, and their mouths and throats were parched and filled with dust.

For a time, the two men disengaged. While they rested, Rustam wondered who his opponent could be. 'There is no doubt of his courage and determination,' he thought ruefully, 'yet he is not known as a champion.'

Refreshed, the warriors continued the battle with bows and arrows, but as each of them wore armour and carried a leopard-skin shield, the arrows' points caused them no injury. Next they fought with clubs, each swinging hefty blows against the other until both fell off their horses. Now they wrestled, and Rustam, fighting like a leopard, pinned Sohrab to the ground. Drawing his dagger, he plunged it deep into his opponent's heart.

As Sohrab lay dying, he said to Rustam, 'My mother gave me tokens by which I might know my father, but my search is over before it has even begun. Perhaps someone will carry to Rustam the news that his son Sohrab has been slain in battle, when his only wish was to find his father.'

On hearing these words, Rustam was filled with dismay. 'What tokens do have you of Rustam?' he demanded.

'Loosen my armour and you will find the amulet tied around my arm, a memento of my father.' Sohrab sighed.

Then Rustam took Sohrab in his arms, and with tears running down his face, confessed his identity to the dying youth and mourned the evil fate that had caused him to kill his only son.

How Ardashir escaped with Golnar

Ardashir was the son of a shepherd called Sasan, who was a descendant of King Darius III. The boy was brought up in obscurity, though Sasan often had dreams about his son's future greatness. Ardashir grew up to be a fine young man. Not only was he exceptionally tall and strong, but he was an excellent horseman and as skilled with his sword as he was in the arts.

Reports of the youth's precocious brilliance attracted the attention of the Persian Shah, Ardavan. The Shah invited Ardashir to court, where the young man proved his prowess at fighting and riding, as well as playing polo and chess. Ardashir soon became a favourite of Ardavan, and this aroused the jealousy of the Shah's son, the Crown Prince.

One day, when Ardashir was hunting with the royal party, he shot an onager, or wild ass, with such skill and force that the arrow passed cleanly through the animal.

'Who has shot down this onager?' Ardavan demanded.

'It was I,' Ardashir replied.

But the Crown Prince said, 'No, it was I who shot it, and now I am looking for its mate.'

Ardashir retorted, 'Then shoot another in the same way. Lying is regarded as a fault in high-born men.'

When he heard this, Ardavan broke into a rage at Ardashir and said, 'The fault is mine, for bringing you to court and including you in my retinue. From now on your place will be in the stables.'

And so Ardavan became a groom. In time, Golnar, the Shah's favourite handmaiden, saw the youth in the stables and fell in love with him. The young couple spent many happy hours together.

After some time had passed, Golnar told Ardashir of a rumour that was circulating the court. 'The astrologers have predicted from the stars the rise of a new ruler. It is said that a male servant who flees from the Shah's court during the next three days will achieve victory, greatness and kingship.'

Ardashir was still angry about the way Ardavan had treated him, so as soon as he heard this news he started to plan their escape.

That night, when the whole palace was asleep, Golnar crept out and opened the door to the treasure house – she took rubies, pearls and as many gold coins as she could carry. Ardashir meanwhile chose two of the finest horses and had them waiting in the stables, ready saddled. As soon as Golnar appeared laden with her spoils, they mounted and galloped out of the palace gates.

On waking, Ardavan found that Golnar was no longer at his side. Courtiers were sent scurrying to find her, and after some time the chief scribe came to the Shah and said, 'Your Majesty, I have to report that last night Golnar and Ardashir fled on two of your Majesty's finest horses.'

Mindful of the astrologers' prediction, Ardavan gave chase. Along the way, he asked everywhere for news of the fugitives.

'They passed through at the speed of a violent wind,' a priest in one village told him. 'They were followed by a fine purple ram as big as a horse, that stirred up the dust as it galloped after them.'

Ardavan knew that the ram was a symbol of the royal glory of Iran. With a sinking heart, he returned to his palace and gathered together an army to fight against Ardashir. However the outcome of the battle was already determined, for Ardashir had taken the royal glory with him.

And so the new Sasanian dynasty of Persia was founded. It was named after Ardashir's father, the shepherd. Golnar became the new Shah's chief wife and gave him fine sons to rule after him.

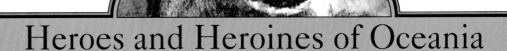

Heroes and Heroines of Oceania

In the countries of Oceania from Australia to Easter Island, tales have been handed down by word of mouth from generation to generation, telling how their ancestral heroes and heroines established the world.

Even today, the past actions of these heroes and heroines affect the lives of their descendants. Caves, rocks and creeks mark the places where their ancestors camped, hunted, fought and loved as they travelled through the land.

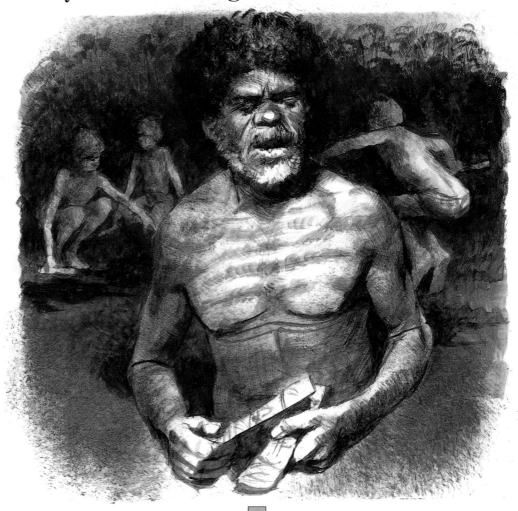

Australia and the Dreamtime

The centre of Australia is criss-crossed by the travelling routes of many ancestral heroes and heroines from the Dreamtime. Some of these ancestors travelled for hundreds of miles, through the lands of many different clans. Each clan recounts the adventures of a particular hero in their area so that a chain of myths stretches across the landscape.

The Dreamtime is both a period of time and a state of being. It refers to the primordial epoch in which the ancestors travelled across Australia, and also how, in the state of Dreaming, a person can become his or her ancestors and recreate their journeys.

THE SEVEN SISTERS

The ancestral heroines known as the Seven Sisters fled south from the centre of Australia to escape from the attentions of a man called Nyiru. The route they took is marked by a string of claypans and rock pools.

At Witapula, the sisters stopped to camp for the night and built a windbreak, which is now a low cliff. The next morning, they dived into the ground, and emerged at a well called Tjuntalitja.

From Tjuntalitja, the Seven Sisters travelled to Wanukuka, where there is a rock hole. At Walinya, they camped again for the night, and their shelter was a cave in a grove of wild fig trees. The place where they sat is marked by some swirling lines in the rock.

Nyiru, who had chased after the sisters, watched from a pile of boulders. When he thought they were asleep, he burst into the cave, gouging the rock as he did so. A low

opening at the back of the cave marks the place where the sisters broke through the wall to escape.

When they reached the coast, the Seven Sisters plunged into the sea. The shock of the cold water made them leap up into the sky, where they became the constellation known as the Pleiades. Nyiru still chases the sisters across the sky. His toes are the belt in the constellation of Orion, and his heel

THE SOUTHERN CROSS

Mululu, leader of the Kanda tribe, had four lovely daughters, but no sons. When he grew old, Mululu worried about the fate of his girls. With no brothers to protect them, he feared they might be forced into marriage with men they disliked, or not receive their share of the game killed by tribal hunters.

Mululu told his daughters that when he died he was going to become a star, and that they should seek the advice of Conduk, the medicine man, about how to join him in heaven.

▷ The Southern Cross is the equivalent constellation in the southern hemisphere to the Plough (otherwise known as the Great Bear) in the northern hemisphere. They are the constellations that people use to find the Pole Star which points due north or south, when travelling at night.

In due course, Mululu died and his daughters set out to find Conduk. He plaited a rope from the hairs of his silver-grey beard, which was so long that one end reached right up into the sky. When the girls climbed up to the top of the rope, they found their father waiting for them. The daughters became the four stars of the Southern Cross. Close by, still caring for them, is their father, the bright star that Europeans know as Centaurus.

THE FIRST SUNRISE

Ancestral heroes are often said to take the shape of animals or birds rather than people. One story of the Australian aboriginals tells how long ago in the Dreamtime, when the ancestral spirits walked the Earth, the sky was so close to the Earth that it blocked out all the light. Everyone had to crawl around on their hands and knees in the dark trying to collect food.

Eventually, the magpies thought of a plan for raising the sky. They gathered some long sticks and used these as levers to lift up the sky, resting it first on low boulders, and then on higher ones.

As the magpies were struggling to raise it high enough for everyone to stand upright, the sky suddenly split open, revealing the first sunrise. The first rays of light broke through the darkness, and the magpies burst into jubilant song. Since then, magpies have always greeted the sunrise with their melodious warbling.

Why the Moon changes his Shape

Long ago, the Moon was always round and bright. Looking down to Earth Bahloo saw many attractive young women, and wanted one to go with him on his lonely journeyings.

One night Bahloo strolled down a deep gorge. His light was hidden until he rounded a cliff – then two girls sitting by the river bank noticed him.

'It's Bahloo, the Moon,' one cried. 'Look how beautiful everything is.'

The Moon puffed up even fatter with pride. He hurried toward the girls on spindly legs, but they hastily jumped into their canoes and paddled away.

'Please don't run away,' Bahloo called after them. 'I won't harm you. I only want you to come with me and live in the sky.'

The girls looked at each other. 'Follow me, I have a plan,' said one to the other. She paddled back to Bahloo's side of the river and jumped ashore.

'Get in my canoe,' she said, 'and we'll tow you across to the other bank.'

Bahloo climbed in and the girls swam alongside. When he looked over the side, he could see his moonlight dancing on their hair and he leaned over to tickle them. One girl dived under the canoe and joined the other.

'Now!' she said, and the two young women tipped the canoe over, spilling the Moon into the water. As he sank, his light dwindled to a silver sliver.

The girls hurried home and told the rest of the tribe what had happened.

Some people were glad at the news, but others were alarmed at the prospect of dark nights to come. They asked Wahn the Crow for his advice.

'Bahloo is not dead,' he told them. 'Look up in the sky – you can still see a tiny piece of him, shining brightly.'

The people looked up and saw a thin slice of light, so pale that it left no shadows on the ground.

'The Moon will get bigger again,' Wahn continued. 'At the moment he is ashamed, but when he regains confidence he'll become as round as he was before. He will try to attract the girls again, but if they take no notice of him he will grow thin in shame once more. And this will happen over and over to the end of time.'

And so it is that the Moon waxes and wanes.

The Islands of the Pacific Ocean

The islands of the Pacific Ocean stretch from Hawaii in the north to New Zealand, and from Easter Island to the Caroline Islands close to the Philippines. Across this enormous area, the same stories are told about the same heroes and heroines, although often the location of the adventure is different.

Maui was the fifth son of Makea-Tutara, chief of the underworld, and of Taranga. One day, Taranga was walking along the seashore when suddenly Maui was born prematurely. Taranga carefully wrapped the unformed body in a lock of her hair and put the bundle in the waves.

The sea fairies found the bundle and hid it in some seaweed. But a storm tore the bundle to pieces and threw the child back on to the beach. There, Maui was found by his own ancestor, Tama-Ranginui, the sun god, who brought him back to life and taught him the lore of his ancestors, including their tales, songs and spells.

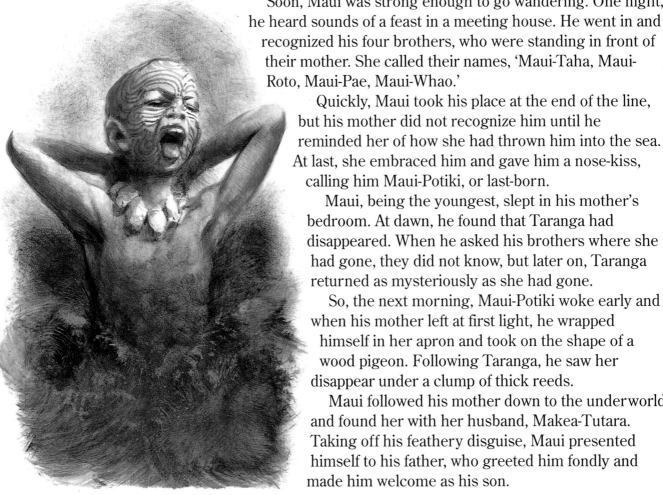

▽ Maui was one of the principal heroes of Polynesian mythology. A trickster and a rebel, he always flouted convention and went against the established order.

Soon, Maui was strong enough to go wandering. One night, he heard sounds of a feast in a meeting house. He went in and recognized his four brothers, who were standing in front of their mother. She called their names, 'Maui-Taha, Maui-Roto, Maui-Pae, Maui-Whao.'

Quickly, Maui took his place at the end of the line, but his mother did not recognize him until he reminded her of how she had thrown him into the sea. At last, she embraced him and gave him a nose-kiss, calling him Maui-Potiki, or last-born.

Maui, being the youngest, slept in his mother's bedroom. At dawn, he found that Taranga had disappeared. When he asked his brothers where she had gone, they did not know, but later on, Taranga returned as mysteriously as she had gone.

So, the next morning, Maui-Potiki woke early and when his mother left at first light, he wrapped himself in her apron and took on the shape of a wood pigeon. Following Taranga, he saw her disappear under a clump of thick reeds.

Maui followed his mother down to the underworld and found her with her husband, Makea-Tutara. Taking off his feathery disguise, Maui presented himself to his father, who greeted him fondly and made him welcome as his son.

How Maui fished up an Island

When he grew older Maui joined his brothers on their fishing expeditions. He was not very good at fishing, but he did enjoy playing tricks on his brothers. Often, just as one of them was pulling in a fish, Maui would jerk it off the line with his own hook and claim it for himself. At last, annoyed by his tricks, Maui's brothers refused to take him fishing with them again.

Maui's mother, Taranga, scolded Maui for not providing her with fish, and eventually his father Makea-Tutara, the chief of the underworld, gave him a fish-hook called Manai-ka-lani, which would provide them with all the fish they needed.

Carrying the special hook, Maui tried to join his brothers next time they went fishing. Calling out that the canoe was too small, they threw him overboard and he had to swim back to land. On that trip, the brothers caught only a shark.

'You would have caught much better fish if I had been with you,' said Maui scornfully.

Finally, the brothers allowed Maui to go out in their canoe, but still they caught only sharks.

'So where are all these fine fish you were talking about?' they asked Maui.

Maui dropped the hook Manai-ka-lani into the sea and chanted an incantation. 'I will bring up the biggest fish you have ever seen,' he boasted.

Just then, the bottom of the sea began to move and the water became violently disturbed. For two days, with the line taut, a huge fish pulled the canoe through the waves. Eventually it tired, and the line slackened.

'Pull hard against it,' Maui commanded his brothers.

This they did, and as they hauled in Maui's line they discovered that it had caught a fish so huge that they cried out in astonishment, 'It is not a fish, but an island!'

With that, the fish broke the line and was lost. But the same thing happened again, and this time Maui was able to grab part of the fish's body, which became Hawaiki island or the North Island of New Zealand. The Maoris call this island Te-ika-a-Maui, or the Fish of Maui.

The canoe was beached on the top of the highest mountain of the island, Mount Hikurangi. Maui's fish-hook became what is now called Hawke Bay.

How Maui brought Fire to his People

In Oceania there are many stories about the bringing of fire to mankind. According to Maori tradition, fire was guarded by an old woman called Mahuika. People called her an ogress, and said, 'She eats human beings like the fire eats wood.'

O ne day, Maui became tired of eating tasteless, raw fish and decided to get some of Mahuika's fire so that he could cook food for himself and his family. He set off in his boat to Mahuika's home in the underworld and waited nearby until she noticed him.

Mahuika had a terrifying appearance, but Maui was not at all frightened. When she came towards him, hands raised menacingly as if she was going to devour him, Maui cried, 'Do not eat me, I am Maui, your grandson.'

Mahuika asked Maui where he came from and who his parents were. When she was satisfied with his answers, she pulled off one of her thick, sharp, fiery nails and gave it to him.

▽ According to Papuan mythology, all the fire on Earth was owned by the Fire Goddess who lived on top of a mountain. The people saw smoke rising from an island in the sea, and so messengers were sent to ask for some of the fire. All failed until finally a dog succeeded in carrying home a stick that was alight at one end.

Maui ran back to his boat with it, but it burned his hands and he dropped it. The fiery nail burned right through the wood of the boat and disappeared into the sea.

So Maui had to go back to the old woman and beg for another nail. This happened several times, until Mahuika finally lost patience and waved her hands at him, saying, 'There, take it all!'

Maui found himself surrounded by fire, and he turned himself into an eagle to escape. But the flames singed his wings dark brown, even as he flew high up in the sky.

Maui then changed into a fish and plunged into the depths of the ocean, but it, too, was boiling hot. Desperately he leaped on to an island and changed himself back into a man. Using a chant he had learned from his father, he called down the rain to put out the fire. Mahuika just managed to save a few sparks by throwing them into the trees as she fled from the tropical storm. And ever since that day, people have made fire from wood.

How Tawhaki married a Goddess

The other great Polynesian hero is Tawhaki. He was the son of Hema and a goddess called Urutonga. One day, Urutonga was captured by some vicious goblins called the Ponaturi, and Hema was taken prisoner while trying to save her. Tawhaki rescued his mother and slaughtered the goblins, who could be killed by sunlight. Then he set out with his brother Kariki to find Hema.

Reaching an island, the brothers came upon their grandmother, the cannibal goddess Whaitiri. She was blind, and they found her carefully counting her baskets of food. Tawhaki took first one and then another basket until he attracted her attention. He then told her who he was and restored her sight by smearing her eyes with clay.

Whaitiri showed the brothers a vine which grew up to heaven. Kariki fell from the vine and was killed, but Tawhaki climbed up and met his ancestors. First, there was Uru Ranginui, god of the winds, and his wife Maikuku. Then, he visited the palace of the war god Maru, who taught him weaponry and the art of chanting spells to paralyze his enemies. Tawhaki also saw the moon and on the beach he met Rongo-Mai, the whale god. Finally, Tawhaki reached the sixth heaven, called Nga-Atua.

Continuing the search for his father, Tawhaki met the goddess Hine Piripiri and fell in love with her. However her cousin, to whom she had been betrothed since childhood, was jealous and planned to kill Tawhaki. He and his fellow murderers left Tawhaki for dead near a pool where he had been bathing. But Hine Piripiri went to look for Tawhaki, found him and nursed him back to health.

When he had recovered, they built a fortified dwelling on a hilltop and there they had a son called Wahieroa. One day, Hine Piripiri's cousin climbed the hill in another attempt to kill his rival. Tawhaki raised his arms and lightning flashed from his armpits, which drove him away. Tawhaki then prayed to his ancestors and they sent torrential rains that destroyed all his enemies.

Heroes and Heroines of Africa

In ancient times, there were many great kingdoms and empires in Africa. Royal rulers were said to be descended from divine beings. The Zulu people of South Africa tell how the High God's son was expelled from heaven because he had stolen the god's favourite cow. The young man was thrown through a hole in the sky with a magical umbilical cord tied round his waist. He became the first king of the Zulus.

Why some Women do no Housework

Among the Luyia of Kenya, some of the women are responsible for special tasks and are freed of the housework that the rest of the women have to do. This is how the situation came about.

In the old days, people did not know how to make pots. To carry water, they used calabashes, which grew wild in the bush. The children saw their mothers carrying the calabashes on their heads and tried to make some play ones with clay.

One day a child's pot got into the fire, and they found that if the clay became hard, the water would not leak out as it did when the pots were wet. So the women copied the children's pots and made bigger pots for their own use. At first these large pots were made of damp clay and they collapsed. They were no use until they had been put in the fire and hardened, as the children had done.

Once, two sisters who lived together fell out over making pots. One sister spent all her time making pots, and left the housework and the water carrying to the other. The second sister was so annoyed about this that she broke all her sister's pots.

Then the pot-maker grew angry and ran away from home. She wandered in the bush for three days until she came to a large lake with a tall tree standing in the middle.

The tree noticed the woman on the bank. It came to her so that she could climb into its branches, then it moved back into the middle again. Meanwhile the woman's parents had been searching everywhere for her. When they reached the lake, they saw their daughter sitting in the tree in the middle of the water. They begged her to return home.

Eventually, the pot-maker agreed to do this if she would be allowed to get on with her work in peace. This is how she became the first woman excused from doing housework.

The Boy who served Death

According to many African peoples there was originally no death, and its arrival is attributed to the actions of human beings or some animal. This is the tradition of the people of Togoland.

Way back in history, there was a great famine in Togoland. A young man was wandering around looking for food when he came to a part of the forest that he had never been in before. In the distance, he could see a strange lump on the ground, and as he got closer he saw that it was a giant. The giant was covered with silky hair, so long that it could have reached from one village to another.

As the young man was creeping quietly away, the giant awoke. 'What do you want?' he bellowed.

'I am hungry. I was just looking for food,' the young man explained.

'If you are willing to be my servant, I will feed you,' said the giant.

The young man learned that the giant's name was Death. He served the giant for some time, and ate his fine food, but eventually became homesick and begged to be allowed to go home.

'You can leave if you promise to send me another servant,' said Death.

The young man went home and sent his brother in his place. But after a time, he was hungry again and longed for some more of the giant's fine

food. So he returned to the forest and was given as much food as he wanted However, he was rather surprised that he never saw his brother at the giant's house. 'Your brother is away on some business,' Death explained.

In time, the young man became homesick again. This time, the giant asked him to send a girl to be his wife, so the young man sent his sister.

Not long after that, the young man was hungry yet again. Death was not pleased to be bothered so frequently. 'Go into the house and get some food for yourself,' he said rather crossly.

Inside the giant's house, the young man picked up a bone with some tender meat on it, and to his horror realized that this was part of his sister.

He ran home at once and gathered together a group of villagers. They crept into the forest and set light to the giant's long hair from a safe distance. The giant tossed and sweated as the flames got closer and closer until he was burned to death.

In the roots of the giant's hair, the young man found a packet of magic powder wrapped up in a leaf.

'Why not try sprinkling it on the bones in the giant's house,' suggested one of the village elders.

When this was done, the young man's brother and sister sprang to life again, laughing with joy for their release.

The young man then proposed putting some of the powder on the giant, but the villagers protested that he, too, might come back to life. However, the young man could not resist sprinkling just a little powder on Death's eye. The eye opened at once, and the villagers ran away in fear.

It is from this time that Death came among men. And every time the giant opens and shuts his eye, another person dies.

How Kintu won Nambi

The kingdom of Buganda lay around Lake Victoria, in what is now Uganda. The Bugandan kings are said to be descended from a great hero called Kintu. He may have been a real historical character, but the stories told about him have been combined with ancient creation myths over the years.

A young man called Kintu arrived in the land that is now Buganda with a single cow and found that there were no other animals or people on Earth. So he lived alone, feeding himself solely on the milk from his cow.

One day, Nambi, the daughter of Gulu, ruler of the sky, came down to Earth and fell in love with Kintu. She wanted to marry him, but her family objected because he was so poor and only had one cow.

'Let us put him to the test,' said Gulu. 'If you boys go and steal his cow, we can see if he survives.'

That night, Nambi's brothers Kaizuku and Walumbe crept down from heaven and took Kintu's cow away. Of course, Kintu no longer had any milk for food, but he managed to survive by eating herbs and leaves.

When Nambi saw that Kintu had passed her father's cruel test she said to the young man, 'My brothers have taken your cow up to heaven. Why don't you come and fetch it?'

Kintu followed Nambi up to heaven and was astonished to see how many houses and how many cows, sheep and chickens there were.

But before he had time to find his cow, Nambi's brothers told their father of his arrival, and Gulu arranged a second test.

A huge meal was cooked, enough to feed over a hundred people. Kintu was imprisoned in a hut alone and told that if he did not eat every scrap he would be killed. After eating as much as he could, Kintu concealed the remainder of the food in a hole in the floor, and then called for servants to come and take away the empty baskets.

The brothers searched every corner of the hut but could find no trace of any food. Convinced that Kintu had tricked him, Gulu

decided
to set Kintu a third test.

'Take this copper axe,' he
ordered, 'and cut me some rocks
for firewood.'

This seemed to Kintu a rather
strange task, but he discovered a
cracked rock and was able to break off some
slivers from it.

Still Gulu was not satisfied, and giving Kintu a
water jug he said, 'Go and fill this jug to the brim
with dew for my morning drink.'

Kintu sat outside all night pondering how he could
fulfil this seemingly impossible task. But early the next
morning, when he picked up the jug, he found to his delight
that it was brimming with dew.

By now, Gulu was very impressed by Kintu's cleverness,
and agreed that he could marry Nambi.

'Go and find your cow,' he said. 'It is pastured with my own cattle.'

Kintu soon realized that this was yet another test, for all of Gulu's cows
looked exactly like his own beast. While he was wondering what to do, a
large bumble bee buzzed in his ear, 'Choose the animal on whose horns I
settle.' Kintu jumped as he recognized Nambi's voice coming from the bee.

On the next morning, when the cows were herded before him, Kintu
watched the bee. While the first herd passed, the bee stayed in a nearby
tree. 'None of those cows are mine,' said Kintu with certainty.

The same thing happened when the second herd was brought, but as the
third was driven past, the bee flew out of the tree and settled on the horns
of a large cow.

'This is my cow,' said Kintu firmly, tapping it on the rump with his stick.

Then the bee flew off and alighted on the horns of three calves, one after
another – two heifers and one bull.

'And these are mine, too, because my cow has given birth to them while
she has been in heaven,' said Kintu.

Gulu was delighted that Kintu had succeeded so well at the fifth test, and
now he welcomed him as his son-in-law.

And so Kintu and Nambi began their journey back to Earth, taking with
them their cows, as well as a sheep, a goat, a hen, a yam plant and a banana
tree. Their descendants became the people of the Bugandan nation.

North America

The legendary hero Hiawatha is credited with bringing peace to the warring Iroquois. Together with another peace-maker called Dekanawideh, he persuaded six Iroquois tribes to form a League of Nations – an idea that was later adopted for the Constitution of the United States.

RAVEN AND THE INUITS

Raven flew down through the darkness and found a new land that he called Earth. He covered it with plants.

One day, Raven noticed a giant pea pod, out of which fell a man, the first Inuit. He created two animals, the musk ox and the caribou, for the man to eat, and then a woman as a companion for the man.

Raven taught the man to build, and the woman how to sew. When they had a child, he told them how to look after it. Three other men then fell from pea pods. Raven created women for them; soon there were many children. But, after a time the people disobeyed Raven. They did not respect the animals and killed more than were needed for food. So Raven went back to the sky.

▽ When Raven returned to the sky, this caused darkness to cover the land once more. But from time to time he allowed the sun to peep through, providing enough light for the people to hunt.

THE BUFFALO STEALER

There was once a great famine among the Blackfoot tribe. For months, the braves had not been able to find buffalo to hunt. In despair, the chief prayed to the creator, Napi, to send them food.

Taking the chief's son with him, Napi set off towards the west. At length the travellers reached a lodge beside a river. 'That is where the buffalo stealer lives,' said Napi. Then he turned himself into a dog, and the youth into a stick.

Soon the wife and son of the buffalo-stealer came by going to the woods, and the boy wanted to take the dog and the stick with him. As Napi was trotting through the wood he saw a buffalo at the mouth of a cave – inside was a whole herd. Napi ran in barking, and the stick drove them out on to the prairie.

When the Blackfoot people saw the buffalo herd, they knew that the chief's prayer had been answered.

The Woman who lived with a Giant

The Inuit peoples live in Alaska and northern Canada on the edge of the Arctic regions of snow and ice. In deepest winter, the day only lasts for two or three hours, so many of their stories are about the sun and fire, or about getting food in a freezing world.

Once upon a time, in the land of the Inuits, there was a man who had an evil temper. The slightest thing made him angry, and he was so feared by everyone in the village that no one dared to go near him.

His poor wife suffered his violence and cruelty until she could bear it no longer. One night, while her husband slept, she packed a small basket of food, pulled on her boots and mittens and crept quietly out of the house.

For several days, the woman walked through the snow towards the icy lands of the far north. She met no one, and soon she had eaten her small supply of food.

Just as she was thinking that she would have to return and face her husband's anger, the woman stumbled upon a recently-killed caribou, half hidden in the snow. 'It must have been left by a hunter who plans to return and collect it later. He won't mind if I eat just a little,' she told herself firmly.

There were a few dry sticks in a hollow at the bottom of a nearby hill, so she built a fire and roasted some of the meat. The food warmed her and gave her strength to continue. Filling her basket with the remainder of the cooked meat, she set off up the hill.

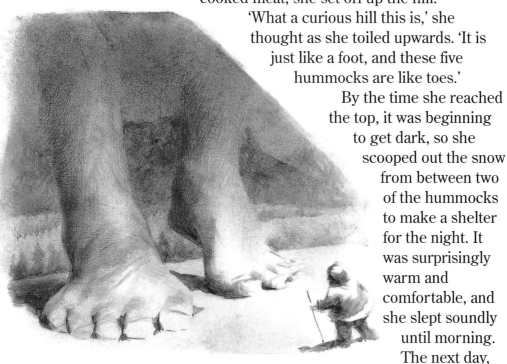

'What a curious hill this is,' she thought as she toiled upwards. 'It is just like a foot, and these five hummocks are like toes.'

By the time she reached the top, it was beginning to get dark, so she scooped out the snow from between two of the hummocks to make a shelter for the night. It was surprisingly warm and comfortable, and she slept soundly until morning. The next day, the woman continued walking northwards along the slope of the hill, and when night fell, she sheltered under a low mound. The following night, she found a deep hollow in the ground, and on the third night, she found herself in a thick forest, where the undergrowth provided a warm and cosy bed.

Next morning, just as she was preparing to set off again, a deep voice bellowed from somewhere overhead. 'Who are you, and what are you doing here?'

Peering upwards, the woman saw a huge glinting eye, and realized with horror that what she had thought was a forest was the beard of an enormous giant! The previous nights had been spent between the giant's toes, under his knee and in his navel.

However, the giant was kindly, and after he had listened to the brave little woman's story, he allowed her to live by the side of his nose, in a hut made of hairs from his beard. There was plenty of food for them both, and she was able to make warm clothing from skins and furs.

The woman was happy enough, but after a time she began to feel homesick. 'I would like to go back,' she confessed to the giant, 'but I am frightened of my husband.'

'There is no need to be frightened,' said the giant gently. 'I will look after you. If you are ever in danger, just call my name, which is Kinak. Now cut off the ear tips of all the skins and furs you have stored and put them in your basket.'

When she had done this, the giant blew her through the air like a feather, right back to her own village. She put the basket of ear tips in the storeroom and went into the house. Her husband, who had grown tired of cooking his own meals, welcomed her back eagerly.

The next morning, when he went to the storeroom, he was astonished to find it full of skins and furs, for every ear tip in the basket had turned into a complete pelt overnight.

The man soon became wealthy, and this improved his temper. For some time, the couple lived happily together, but in time, the husband returned to his old ways and began to beat his wife and treat her harshly again.

The woman remembered what the giant had said and called out, 'Kinak, Kinak, help me!' Immediately, the sky grew dark with thunderclouds and a fierce whirlwind lifted the man high up into the air and carried him away out of sight, never to be seen again.

Hiawatha, the Peacemaker

The legends told about this Native American chief inspired the American poet Henry Wadsworth Longfellow to write *The Song of Hiawatha*. One of the most exciting parts of this very long poem deals with his chase after the wicked Pau-Puk Keewis.

The Iroquois nation revelled in war, and different Iroquois tribes were always fighting each other. Sometimes they joined forces to fight their neighbours, the Algonquin, and both these great nations spent much of their time and energy in plotting or waging war. But in one of the Iroquois tribes, known as the Mohawks, there was a chief who believed in peace, not war. His name was Hiawatha.

Hiawatha had seven daughters whom he loved dearly, and of whom he was very proud. One by one, these daughters mysteriously died, poisoned by sorcery. Hiawatha was so distraught that he decided to leave his tribe and go to visit the shamans of the spirit land. The wisdom that Hiawatha acquired from them taught him that war leads only to misery.

The shamans gave Hiawatha a magic canoe that transported him between the world of the spirits and the world of men. All the Iroquois people came to revere Hiawatha, except for Tadodaho, a chief of the Onondaga tribe. He was a powerful sorcerer who could kill men with his magic, but could not be destroyed himself. His body was distorted by seven crooks and his hair was a nest of rattlesnakes. Tadodaho opposed Hiawatha violently and spoke against him at tribal meetings.

One day, a Huron chief called Dekanawideh crossed Lake Ontario in a canoe and came to the territory of the Mohawk people. A Mohawk warrior saw him quietly smoking and meditating at the base of a tall tree, and reported his arrival.

When the chiefs and headmen went out to question him, Dekanawideh gave them this message, 'The Creator from whom we are all descended has sent me to establish a league of peace among you. The tribes will stop warring, and you will no longer kill one another. War is evil, and your Creator forbids it. Peace and comfort are much better than war and misery for a nation.'

Hiawatha made Dekanawideh welcome, and agreed to try and persuade the Mohawk people to proceed with his plan for peace. Dekanawideh presented Hiawatha with five beautiful strings of shells, saying, 'The grief you have suffered is terrible, but I give you these to clear your mind.'

The two peace-makers then began to spread the idea of the league of peace, and won over the chiefs of the Oneida, Cayuga and Seneca tribes. The great majority of the Onondaga chiefs were also won over, but Tadodaho remained unconvinced. Without his support, the league could not become a reality. He agreed only when it was established that he would be supreme chief over all the league.

Then, at a great council, Hiawatha straightened the kinks out of the sorcerer's body and combed the rattlesnakes from his hair. The name Hiawatha means 'comber', and comes from this great deed of power.

When Hiawatha was satisfied that the tribes would live peacefully together, he paddled away in his magic canoe to join his beloved daughters in the land of the spirits. He thought the people on Earth had no more need of him and so he burned his canoe. But once the great peacemaker had left, the Iroquois soon returned to their warlike ways.

One day Hiawatha came back from a hunting expedition, only to find that Pau-Puk Keewis, the crafty wizard, had been causing havoc in the village where they both lived.

Pau-Puk Keewis had been Hiawatha's friend and had danced at his wedding. But now he had persuaded the young men to gamble at Bowl and Counters, and had won all their weapons, pipes and deerskin shirts. Then he had entered Hiawatha's wigwam and thrown everything into disorder.

Hiawatha and some other Iroquois set off in hot pursuit of the mischief-maker, following his trail through the forest. But Pau-Puk Keewis had already reached a beaver's lodge in the river and transformed himself into an enormous beaver – ten times larger than the others.

Hiawatha and his hunters leapt on to the roof of the lodge and trapped Pau-Puk Keewis inside. With their clubs they beat him to death and carried his body home on a stretcher of poles and branches.

But the ghost of Pau-Puk Keewis whirled off through the pine trees. First it transformed itself into a huge duck and then into a serpent. Finally Pau-Puk Keewis, once again in human form, was given shelter in the deep caverns of the Old Man of the Mountain. But Hiawatha managed to destroy him by calling down the thunder and lightning to split the mountain open.

That was the end of the wicked Pau-Puk Keewis, but his name still lives on. In winter, when the snowflakes whirl in eddies round the wigwams, people say that Pau-Puk Keewis is dancing through the village.

There are hundreds of books about the heroes and heroines of the world and their doings. Go and look in your local library or your nearest bookshop and you will find a good choice of books to investigate. The following list includes some collections that you should look out for and some books for adults which you might find interesting.

A good collection of myths and legends from around the world can be found in the Oxford University Press's (OUP) series: OXFORD MYTHS & LEGENDS.

Children's books that will tell you more

Favourite North American Indian Legends, Philip Smith (Dover Publications).

Folktales and Fables of the Americas and the Pacific, Molly Perham and Robert Ingpen (Dragon's World).

Folktales and Fables of Asia and Australia, Molly Perham and Robert Ingpen (Dragon's World).

Folktales and Fables of Europe, Molly Perham and Robert Ingpen (Dragon's World).

Folktales and Fables of the Middle East and Africa, Molly Perham and Robert Ingpen (Dragon's World).

The Great Deeds of Superheroes, Maurice Saxby and Robert Ingpen (Dragon's World).

King Arthur & the Legends of Camelot, Molly Perham & Julek Heller (Dragon's World)

Legends of Charlemagne, Thomas Bulfinch (Everyman Library, Dent)

The Luck of Troy, Roger Lancelyn Green (Puffin).

Myths of the Norsemen, Roger Lancelyn Green (Puffin).

Sinbad the Sailor, and other tales from the Arabian Nights, N.J. Dawood (Puffin).

Tale of Troy, Roger Lancelyn Green (Puffin).

Tales of Ancient Egypt, Roger Lancelyn Green (Puffin).

Tales of the Arabian Nights, Amabel Williams-Ellis (Blackie)

Tales of the Greek Heroes, Roger Lancelyn Green (Puffin).

A Treasury of Giant and Monster Stories, A. Spenceley (illustrator) (Kingfisher).

Adult books you might enjoy

Aboriginal Mythology, Nyoongah (Aquarian Press).

Dragons, Gods & Spirits from Chinese Mythology, Tao Tao Liu Saunders (Peter Lowe).

Encyclopedia of Things That Never Were, Michael Page and Robert Ingpen (Dragon's World).

Epic of the Kings (Shah-nama), Ferdowsi (Routledge).

Gods, Demons and Others, R.K. Narayan (Mandarin).

Kings, Gods & Spirits from African Mythology, Jan Knappert (Peter Lowe).

The Mahabarata, R.K. Narayan (Mandarin).

Myths and Legends of China, E.T.C. Werner (Dover Publications).

Myths and Legends of Japan, F. Hadland Davis (Dover Publications).

Orlando Furioso, Ariosto (trs Guido Waldman) (Oxford University Press).

The Ramayana, R.K. Narayan (Vision Press).

Sir Gawain and the Green Knight, B. Stone (Penguin).

The Song of Hiawatha, Henry Wadsworth Longfellow (Wordsworth).

Spirits, Heroes & Hunters from North American Indian Mythology, Marion Wood (Peter Lowe).

Warriors, Gods & Spirits from Central & South American Mythology, Douglas Gifford (Peter Lowe).